The PRAYING LIFE

LIVING BEYOND YOUR LIMITS

JENNIFER KENNEDY DEAN

New Hope
Birmingham, Alabama

New Hope
P. O. Box 12065
Birmingham, Alabama 35202-2065

Cover design by Janell E. Young

Dewey Decimal Classification: 248.3
Subject Headings: PRAYER
　　　　　　　　　CHRISTIAN LIFE
　　　　　　　　　PRAYER—BIBLICAL TEACHING

ISBN: 1-56309-091-0
N944105•0294•5M1

This book is dedicated to
Wayne, my husband, partner, friend
and to our sons,
Brantley, Kennedy, and Stinson

You are the best part of my life.

Thanks to

My parents, Don and Audrey Kennedy, for living prayer and for never giving up on me.

My sisters, Priscilla Graham and Julianne Pederson, for unlimited support and encouragement.

My friend, Karin Robertson, for typing, suggesting, and praying.

My uncle, the late Jack Tohtz, for editing my manuscript and challenging my thinking.

My editor, Becky Nelson, for working hard to make this book the best it could be.

The artist, Janell Young, for using her talents to make the message of *The Praying Life* clearer than words alone could make it.

Contents

INTRODUCTION

I grew up in a praying family. From earliest childhood, I was encouraged to commit everything to God through prayer. Nothing was either too insignificant or too important to leave in God's hands. My parents did not teach me how to pray with their words only but also with their lives. They had more than "a prayertime," a section of their days set aside for praying. Prayer permeated and controlled every aspect of their lives. That is what the phrase *the praying life* means to me.

When I became a young adult, I realized that a praying life was not built only on information communicated from one person to another but on a life-absorbing relationship with God. I sensed the difference between a *prayer life* and a *praying life*, and I knew which I wanted. But there was only One Who could teach me to pray the way I wanted to pray. To Him I brought my inadequacy and my hungry heart. I confessed that while I knew how to say prayers, I did not know how to pray. I asked Him to teach me. This book is a record of what I have learned.

God began to open His Word to me in a new way. Familiar passages took on fresh meaning. Dull, dry passages pulsed with new life. Each time I discover a prayer concept in His Word, He brings me opportunities to put it into practice. The words of the Scriptures shape my life and define my experiences. Slowly but surely, He is building a praying life.

As I submitted myself to God for instruction in prayer, He seemed to ask me, "Why do you want to learn to pray?" I knew all the right answers, but they sounded strangely hollow. My experience must have been similar to Peter's. How surprised he was when Jesus did not accept his glib and easy answer to the question, "Peter, do you love me?" Each time Jesus repeated the question, Peter must have been forced to look deeper inside his heart for the true answer. God peeled back my layers of practiced answers as He did Peter's.

I finally admitted the truth. "I want to know how to get God to do what I want Him to do when I want Him to do it. I hope to learn how to make use of prayer for my benefit." Once I reached that point of honesty, I knew my course was set. God could work with me now because He could begin with my weakness. God could begin by teaching me a new *purpose* for praying.

The Praying Life is the record of my journey up to now. It is my hope that in recording what I have learned and the inner changes that have occurred, others will be inspired to sit at the Master's feet.

SECTION 1

THE PURPOSE OF
PRAYER

The purpose of prayer is not to change God, but to allow Him to change us. It is to discover and do God's will, not to obligate Him to do ours. The purpose of prayer is that God's splendor will be displayed on earth as it is in heaven.

The first issue to be resolved was: Can I change God through prayer? I had to be clear on this point because much of my prayertime had been spent dealing with God as if I could change Him. I prayed as if I could open God's eyes to new possibilities, awaken mercy or love in Him, or sway Him to my point of view. I approached prayer as if God were selfishly hoarding blessings and my role was to convince Him to release a few. It was a draining responsibility—having to be clever enough, fervent enough, or persistent enough to convince God. It caused my prayer life to be anxiety-driven, always wondering if I had been effective enough to win God over.

Balak, king of the Moabites (Num. 22–24), tried to change God's mind and did not give up easily. He tried to hire God's prophet Baalam to curse the Israelites, whom God had blessed. He made five attempts to get God to see his point of view. He was persistent, determined to get God to perform for him. God's answer to Balak, delivered through Baalam, was this: "'God is not a man, that he should lie, nor a son of man, that he should change his mind. Does he speak and then not act? Does he promise and not fulfill? I have received a command to bless; he has blessed, and I cannot change it'" (Num. 23:19-20).

King Saul learned a similar truth. The prophet Samuel delivered God's command to Saul about how to dispose of the Amalekites (1 Sam. 15). Saul disobeyed God and listened to the desires of the people instead. "'I have sinned. I violated the Lord's command and your instructions. I was afraid of the people and so I gave in to them'" (1 Sam. 15:24). As a result, God rejected him as king over Israel. God delivered this message to Saul through Samuel: "'He who is the Glory of Israel does not lie or change his mind; for he is not a man, that he should change his mind'" (1 Sam. 15:29).

In both these instances, God delivered a straightforward message. He does not change His mind. His purposes are fixed and cannot be altered by men. Persuasive or clever speech has no influence on God.

Yet on other occasions God seemed to change His mind in response to man's intercession. In the story recorded in Exodus 32:9-14, the Israelites angered God by building a golden calf to represent Jehovah in worship. God declared that as a result of their idolatry, He would destroy them and make a great nation of Moses. Moses prayed, "'Turn from your fierce anger; relent and do not bring disaster on your people'" (Ex. 32:12). Exodus 32:14 says, "Then the Lord relented and did not bring on his people the disaster he had threatened." How can we reconcile the sovereign and unchangeable purposes of God with the intercession of His people?

Israel and the Golden Calf

If God changed His mind in response to Moses' prayer to spare the Israelites, does that mean that Moses was more merciful than God? Does it mean that Moses taught God a lesson in forgiveness? Does it mean that Moses helped God cool His anger so that He would not do something He would ultimately regret? Was Moses' wisdom greater than God's? Does God make rash decisions in the heat of anger and later repent? If so, then God is not Who He claims to be.

Was it Moses' character that influenced God where others could not? If so, Moses' prayers should always have been answered affirmatively, but they were not. In the instance reported by Moses in Deuteronomy 3:26, Moses says, "But because of you the Lord was angry with me, and would not listen to me; 'That is enough,' the Lord said. 'Do not speak to me any more about this matter.'" Moses had tried to change God's mind about letting him enter the Promised Land. Surely Moses was more deserving of God's mercy than the Israelites had been after building a golden calf. God changed His mind about destroying Israel, but would not change His mind about Moses' entering the Promised Land.

Or is this the way it happened? God, in His sovereignty and infinite wisdom, decides it is best to destroy the Israelites because of their idolatry. Moses makes a passionate plea on their behalf. God listens, then decides, "Moses has a point there. I hadn't thought of it like that. I'll change My mind and do it Moses' way."

How can we reconcile the sovereignty of God with the intercession of His people? 4-10-95 \ 1:20 am.

Judah's Unfaithfulness and Israel's Idolatry

We begin to see the truth when we compare this occurrence to a similar occurrence with a different outcome. Compare the Israelites' standing before God after the worship of the golden calf with that of the nation of Judah just before Babylonian captivity described in Ezekiel 22.

In Ezekiel 22, God lists His people's sins against Him. They had broken covenant and deserved judgment because the wages of sin is death. The Israelites also deserved judgment for breaking covenant and worshiping an image. They also had incurred God's wrath and brought judgment upon themselves.

Yet, in both instances, God desired to show mercy. In Moses' story, would God's true purpose have been accomplished by destroying Israel? And did Moses dissuade Him then? No. His original purpose, His true purpose, was to preserve Israel. God had told Moses that He would destroy Israel and make a great nation from Moses. God had prophesied that the Messiah would come through the tribe of Judah. Moses was from the tribe of Levi. Did God want to destroy the tribe that was to produce the Messiah?

In the story of Judah we see God's desire forthrightly stated: "So I would not have to destroy it." God did not want the people to receive what they had earned.

In both instances, then, the people have brought upon themselves God's righteous judgment. In both cases, God's desire is to circumvent the natural course of events (sin earns death) and show mercy. In both instances, God looks for an intercessor.

In Moses' story, God said this to Moses: "'Go down, because your people, whom you brought up out of Egypt, have become corrupt. . . . I have seen these people . . . and they are a stiff-necked people. Now leave me alone so that my anger may burn against them. Then I will make you into a great nation'" (Ex. 32:7-10).

What was God telling Moses? God refers to the Israelites as "your people." He was reminding Moses that God had appointed him as the leader of these people, which includes a call to be their intercessor. These people were Moses' God-appointed responsibility.

Then God told Moses what the people had brought upon themselves. He showed Moses the reason that intercession was called for.

Finally, He brought to the forefront Moses' selfless love for the people and his loyalty to the eternal purpose of God. "'Then I will make you into a great nation,'" God told Moses. To a person motivated by personal ambition, this would have been an attractive offer. To Moses, whose heart and mind were God's, this would have derailed God's eternal plan. Moses was so aligned with God's purposes and so identified with the objects of his intercession that God's statements to him were a call to intercede.

In Judah's story, we know God looked for an intercessor because Ezekiel 22:30 says: "'I looked for a man among them'" to intercede.

The critical difference was, the idolatrous Israelites had an intercessor and sinful Judah had none. Ezekiel 22:30-31 says: "'I looked for a man among them who would build up the wall and stand before me in the gap on behalf of the land so I would not have to destroy it, but I found none. So [i.e., not because they've sinned, but because there is no intercessor] I will pour out my wrath on them and consume them with my fiery anger, bringing down on their own heads all they have done, declares the Sovereign Lord.'"

When God looked for an intercessor for the Israelites, He found Moses. He found someone through whom He could pour out His mercy, someone whose heart would match His. When God looked for an intercessor for Judah, He found no one. Israel received mercy. Judah received judgment.

If God had destroyed the nation of Israel, He would have had to change His mind about His eternal plan. He would have had to deny His own nature, showing Himself to be changeable and volatile. We would have seen a God Who made a spur-of-the-moment decision to override an eternal course. Look at the following chart comparing the two situations.

Israel: Exodus 32	Judah: Ezekiel 22
Breaks covenant with God. (vv. 1-4)	Breaks covenant with God. (vv. 23-29)
Deserves judgment. (v. 8)	Deserves judgment. (v. 31)
God desires mercy. (Gen. 49:10—God wants to preserve Messiah's tribe.)	God desires mercy. (v. 30)
God looks for intercessor. (vv. 7-10)	God looks for intercessor. (v. 30)
God finds Moses. (v. 11)	God finds no one. (v. 30)
Israel receives mercy. (v. 14)	Judah receives judgment. (v. 31)

Moses did not *change* God's mind, He *shared* God's mind. He did not alter God's plan, he implemented it.

From a one-dimensional point of view, it appeared that Moses had changed God's mind. Instead, through His intercession, Moses reflected God's love and redemptive purposes. The Bible is the record of God's work in and through people. God reveals His character as He relates to real human beings in real circumstances. In this particular circumstance, God showed that He will do His work through intercessors. To overrule judgment, God must have someone available and willing to intercede for mercy, opening the way for God to do what He longs to do. When He found no such person in Judah, the people suffered the full consequences of their actions. The different outcomes, mercy as opposed to judgment, hinged on the availability of an intercessor. This concept will be expanded upon and clarified throughout this book.[1]

God's Purpose for Prayer

Through prayer, then, God accomplishes His purposes. The purpose of prayer, I learned, is not to change God, but to allow Him to change me. The purpose of prayer is to discover God's will, not obligate Him to do mine; to reflect God's mind, not change it. I could, through prayer, release God's mercy to bring about the best possible solution in every situation. Jeremiah 29:11 says: "'For I know the plans I have for

you,' declares the Lord, 'plans to prosper you and not to
harm you, plans to give you hope and a future.'" Could I
learn, like Moses, to make my heart available for God's purposes?

My first step, finding a new purpose for prayer, would require an inner transformation. Changing my prayer focus
from my own satisfaction and happiness to God's glory and
eternal purposes would take a brand-new heart. God
promised just such a drastic reorientation in Ezekiel 36:26-27:
"'I will give you a new heart and put a new spirit in you . . . .
And I will put my Spirit in you and move you to follow my
decrees and be careful to keep my laws.'" God had already
promised to reproduce His heart in me so that I would want
what He wants to give. He promised to take my self-centered
heart and fasten it on Him.

Personal Prayer Experience

Let the loving presence of God envelop you. Acknowledge
that He knows every thought and intention of your heart.
Nothing is hidden from Him. Instead of feeling exposed or
vulnerable, you can feel safe and protected. Remember that
He is kind, tenderhearted, forgiving, and trustworthy.

Tell Him about your desire to enter into a deeper relationship with Him. Tell Him all your misgivings—all the times
you've tried and failed, the pieces of your life you really don't
want Him to have, your sense of inadequacy, your selfish
motives, the fear that you will discover that the praying life
doesn't really work. Put all your misgivings in His strong
hands.

Ask Him to teach you to pray. Visualize looking into the
precious face of Jesus. Listen as He tells you of the joy He
feels because you have put yourself in His hands. Listen to
His assurance that He will not fail you.

Don't hurry. Take all the time you need.

THE DEFINITION OF PRAYER

To bring my prayers into alignment with His purposes, I had to redefine prayer completely. If prayer is not for the purpose of moving God to my point of view, what is prayer? If I can't change God, why should I pray?

A new definition of prayer began to emerge in my life and thinking. Prayer is not a group of words sandwiched between "Dear God" and "Amen." It is not begging, pleading, convincing, or twisting God's arm. Prayer is not a way to get God to do what we want Him to do when we want Him to do it. I had been telling God what to do, expressed in religious-sounding words, and expecting Him to obey me. When He didn't obey me, I was disappointed in Him. Prayer, I learned, is not expecting God to carry out my decisions. Prayer is not giving God instructions to follow.

"To pray is to let Jesus glorify His name in the midst of our needs," says O. Hallesby in his book *Prayer*. Prayer is simply opening our lives to God, acknowledging our total dependence on Him. Prayer is not limited to a segment of our lives or to a scheduled event in our days. It is an attitude of receptivity and openness which permeates our lives and to which God responds eagerly. It is living in the presence of God, always in the process of being reshaped and re-created by Him.

Through prayer, God wants to make us partakers of His divine nature (2 Pet. 1:4). He wants to reproduce His heart in us. Oswald Chambers, in his book *Christian Disciplines,* says, "Prayer . . . is the means whereby we assimilate more and more of His mind." The primary goal of prayer is not to tell God what is on our minds, but to listen to what is on His. It is not placing the desires of our hearts on His, but His placing the desires of His heart on ours. The main purpose of prayer is to understand the heart of God and cooperate with the purposes of God.

God initiates prayer. We need waste no time trying to get God's attention. God's attention has never wandered from us. His heart is set on us to do us good. It is His divine wooing that has awakened our desire to seek Him. In every circumstance, the Holy Spirit, Who knows the mind of God, will teach us to pray as we ought, will shape our prayers, will pray through us. Little by little, under His loving tutelage, we will find our prayers reflecting God's will.

The lesson to be learned in prayer is how to love and enjoy God, how to know Him by experience. Through constant exposure to Him, we learn to live with God as our reference point. All of life—every experience, every relationship, every problem—is evaluated in light of His eternal wisdom.

The Immediate Versus the Ultimate

We must learn to give up our tendency to see God's complete will and God's best in isolated blocks. God will work out His will according to an eternal strategy. Each individual circumstance will be one little piece of the big plan. We tend to try to define God's will incident by incident, happening by happening, as if each occurrence in our lives stands alone. Instead, everything is being blended together into the whole. "The Lord works out everything for his own ends" (Prov. 16:4). We shouldn't focus our faith on a specific outcome to a specific incident, but on God's eternal plan. We must learn to watch for how the immediate flows into the ultimate.

What happens when we see our lives in little blocks? We reach this conclusion: "I prayed and prayed about this, but still this terrible thing happened. This can't be God's will. I'll have to find a new way to get God's will accomplished." We must learn to see God's actions in our lives in response to our prayers as an ongoing eternal strategy instead of many little isolated plans. The following illustration will help you see the difference:

Our one-dimensional view of God's will:

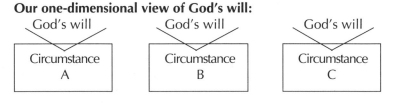

God's eternal view:

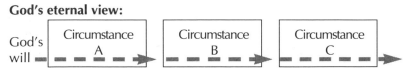

Living Prayer Brings a Changed Heart

By living every moment in His presence, we are gradually changed into the likeness of His Son, Who is the exact representation of His nature (Heb. 1:3). The Father and the Son are one (John 10:30). We cannot be in the presence of God without being in the presence of Jesus. We cannot behold Jesus without beholding God.

Second Corinthians 3:18 says: "And we, who with unveiled faces all reflect the Lord's glory, are being transformed into his likeness with ever-increasing glory, which comes from the Lord, who is the Spirit." The natural result of being with Jesus is change. We are not changing ourselves, we are being changed. We are transformed by the indwelling Spirit. We are changed so completely that we reflect Him.

If we focus on ourselves, trying to effect change by our own efforts, we'll always stay the same. If our attention is focused on Jesus, we begin to absorb and then reflect Him. If there were a mirror in which to see our inner reflections, we would look into that mirror and see Jesus reflected there. We would be reflections of His glory.

This transformation happens gradually. It requires time, a precious commodity in this instant age. It requires commitment. We will have to give up some of the activities that fill our days and the thoughts that fill our minds. In focusing on Him, we are changed by the Holy Spirit. Slowly, God accomplishes what He wants: a heart that reflects His. This is the goal of the praying life.

Living in a Love Relationship with God

Do you wonder how you will find the time for such total devotion? Does it sound as if God is calling upon you to live a cloistered life, oblivious to the many practical demands of day-to-day living? The praying life requires no such thing! With the Holy Spirit as your guide, you will discover a deeper level of living and responding. You are always involved in thinking and feeling, aren't you? You will learn to make God the focal point of your unceasing thought processes and find yourself involved in unceasing prayer.

Living by the Spirit

The praying life means living by your spiritual nature rather than by your human nature. Your human nature is dictated to and enslaved by your physical senses. Your spiritual nature, your inner man, is attuned to and directed by God. Your spiritual nature is God Himself indwelling you, giving life to your spirit. "Those who live in accordance with the Spirit have their minds set on what the Spirit desires. . . . The mind controlled by the Spirit is life and peace" (Rom. 8:5-6).

Living by your human nature means limiting yourself. Sin reigns in your mortal body and your human nature obeys its demands (see Rom. 6:12). Your body is the vehicle through which you experience the physical world. You are alive to the physical world through your body. If your physical body was dead, you would not feel the pull of your physical needs and desires. The physical world would mean nothing to you because you would have no connection to it.

Your body and the physical world are not bad. They are God's wonderful creations. Your physical needs and the needs of your human nature are not wrong. God created you with needs and He uses your needs to draw you to Him. He has created you with needs for which He alone is the answer. However, a law of sin is at work in your human nature (Rom. 7:23,25), which causes you to try to get your God-created needs met outside of God. The law of sin at work in your life is what leads to sinful actions. The law of sin influences you to act in ways contrary to your best interest. The law of sin rules in your body and influences you to sin against God.

"The sinful mind [mind controlled by human nature] is hostile to God. It does not submit to God's law, nor can it do so. Those controlled by the sinful nature cannot please God" (Rom. 8:7-8).

Just as your body is the vehicle through which you experience the physical world, your spirit is the vehicle through which you experience God. Apart from God, you cannot feel the pull of your spiritual needs or experience the truth of the spiritual world. Just as God raised Jesus from the dead physically, He gave life to your spirit (see Eph. 2:4-5). Now you are the person you were created to be. Now you are freed from the law of sin because of an overriding law, the law of the Spirit (see Rom. 8:2). You are now dead to sin (not responsive to its pull) and alive to God (see Rom. 6:11). "You, however, are controlled not by the sinful nature but by the Spirit, if the Spirit of God lives in you" (Rom. 8:9).

Now you have a choice. You can live by the dictates of your human nature, which are opposed to God's rule; or by the guidance of the Spirit of God, alive in your innermost being. The praying life is a life lived in the Spirit; a life always in communion with God, ruled by the Spirit, not by the human nature. The following chart will summarize the two natures and the manifestations of each.

Human Nature	Spiritual Nature
Ruled by law of sin. (Rom. 7:23)	Ruled by Spirit. (Rom. 8:6)
Hostile to God. (Rom. 8:8)	At peace with God. (Rom. 8:1)
Unable to submit to God's laws . (Rom. 8:7)	Free to submit to God's law . (Rom. 8:2)
Destructive. (Rom. 8:6,13)	Restorative. (Rom. 8:13)
Unfulfilled, frustrated. (Rom. 7:23)	Fulfilled, satisfied. (Rom. 7:25–8:1)
Dead to God, alive to sin. (Eph. 2:1-2)	Alive to God, dead to sin. (Rom. 6:7,11)

Which do you prefer? Which do you believe would lead to life and peace? Which would be the most productive, life-enhancing way to live.

Personal Prayer Experience

List your most urgent prayer requests. In each case, write out your expectations of God.

Now close your eyes and visualize yourself kneeling before Jesus on His throne. In your own way, worship Him and affirm that He is Lord.   `/· 57`

One by one, present your requests before Him. Tell Him specifically each expectation that you are surrendering. Ask Him to replace your expectations with His desires. Take your time. Wait after each expectation is surrendered until you know in your spirit that you have truly let your expectations go. He may begin at that moment to re-create your desires or He may do it over the days and weeks to come. Don't become anxious about it. He is faithful.

Record His answers as they come so that you will be encouraged to turn other things over to God.

THE NECESSITY OF PRAYER

Although prayer does not change God's will, it does activate God's will. God's plan for our individual lives will not be all that it can be unless we pray. Prayer releases the power of God to accomplish the will of God in situations and in the lives of people. Prayer is the channel through which God's will is brought to earth. He has a veritable flood of mercies which are dammed up because there is no prayer to open the floodgates.

Jesus taught His disciples to pray, "Thy will be done in earth, as it is in heaven." In other words, let Your will be done on earth just like it's already done in heaven. God's will, or plan, is available for every person and situation on earth. There is a gap, however, between what God wills in heaven and what is happening on earth. God describes intercession as standing in the gap, or making up the breach (see Ezek. 22:30 and Psalm 106:23). As intercessors, we stand in that gap linking heaven's plan and earth's circumstances.

Standing in the Gap

What is the gap, or the breach? It seems to me that when God first created the world, there was no gap. "God saw all that he had made, and it was very good" (Gen. 1:31). God was pleased and satisfied with things on the earth. God's will was fully executed on the earth. When sin entered the picture, a gap was created. God's perfect will was no longer in effect on the earth. Now there was a gap between what God desired for earth and what was so on earth.

God's will is already done in heaven. All the promises of God are already yes in Jesus. He has things prepared and waiting for us that are beyond our ability to imagine. Prayer brings the will of God, the things God has prepared and waiting for us in heaven, to earth. Through prayer we stand in the gap and make up the breach before Him.

Through prayer the decrees of God, forever established in heaven, flow to earth. The following illustrations will help you understand this concept. Look at illustration A. Let the dry cell represent God's power. Nothing needs to be added to it. It is ready and waiting. Let the light bulb represent a need on earth. The question is, how do we get the power to the need?

ILLUSTRATION A
Question: How do we get the power to the need?

Question in prayer: Not How can I get God to do something? but How can I get what God has already done from heaven onto earth?

Need

DRY CELL

Source of power: God

Now look at illustration B. The power begins to flow toward the need by means of a wire. When the power (electricity) reaches a gap, the electricity cannot jump over the gap. Electricity cannot jump over air, but requires a conductor. This does not mean that the power is diminished or unavailable, but that it must be conducted through the gap.

ILLUSTRATION B

Problem: Electricity cannot jump over air, but must be conducted through the gap.

Problem in prayer: God's power cannot jump over the gap created by sin and must be conducted through the gap. The problem is not how to get God to care more or how to get God to come up with a solution but how to conduct the power of God through the gap.

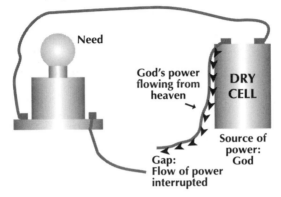

Finally, look at illustration C. When a conductive substance is placed in the gap, the electricity can complete its circuit. The same principle applies when God's power begins to flow out of heaven to earth. It comes to the gap. As an intercessor stands in the gap, the flow of God's power continues through the gap and reaches the need. Now the need becomes a reflection of the power of God.

ILLUSTRATION C

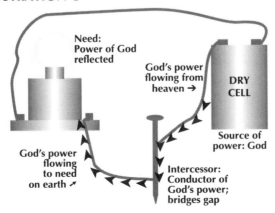

In Matthew 18:18 (NASB), Jesus says, "'Truly I say to you, whatever you shall bind on earth shall have been bound in heaven; and whatever you loose on earth shall have been loosed in heaven.'" The verb tenses indicate that it happens in heaven first. Prayer does not change that which has already been done in heaven, but releases it. Prayer begins in heaven, where God's plan is in full effect. When you pray, God does not begin at that moment to search for a solution. He begins at that moment to release the solution already fully developed in heaven.

Daniel's Example

Observe the intercession of Daniel. Daniel read the writings of the prophet Jeremiah and saw that the time allotted for the desolation of Jerusalem was coming to an end; the completion of the desolations was at hand. What did he do? He began to pray. He saw God's heart, God's revealed will, and he began to pray toward that end. "In the first year of his reign, I, Daniel, understood from the Scriptures, according to the word of the Lord given to Jeremiah the prophet, that the desolation of Jerusalem would last seventy years. So I turned to the Lord God and pleaded with him in prayer and petition, in fasting, and in sackcloth and ashes" (Dan. 9:2-3).

What was the purpose of Daniel's prayer? He was not informing God. He was not trying to shape God's will. Daniel's prayer was in response to God's initiative. God had already determined when the desolation of Jerusalem would end. He revealed His intentions to Daniel through the Scriptures. Daniel did not assume that God's will would come to pass without his prayers. He knew that once God's heart had been revealed to him, he was to respond by praying. Daniel's prayers would activate God's expressed will. God's Word tells us exactly what we can expect of God if we ask Him.

God Waits for Our Prayers

God's answers are predicated upon a request being made. "'Call to me and I will answer you and tell you great and unsearchable things you do not know'" (Jer. 33:3). "'He will call upon me, and I will answer him'" (Psalm 91:15). "'Ask and it will be given to you'" (Matt. 7:7). "'And I will do whatever you ask in my name'" (John 14:13). God wants our prayers. He waits for our prayers. He has chosen to condition the demonstration of His power on our prayers.

Why would God ordain prayer as the appointed way of accomplishing His will? Wouldn't He avoid much trouble if He did just what He wanted to do, apart from our interference?

The reason for prayer is that God wants relationship. We were created for friendship and fellowship with Him. God wants us to be participants in His kingdom, not observers. Through prayer God wants to reproduce His heart in us and allow us to rule with Christ. Through prayer He allows us to take part in establishing His kingdom. Ephesians 1:20 explains that Christ is seated at the right hand of God. Ephesians 2:6 states that we are seated there with Him. Jesus has purchased a place of honor for us and has offered us the opportunity to unite with Him in His spiritual rule from the right hand of God. He makes the decisions and we implement them through prayer. Our prayers enforce His rule and authority.

In response to our prayers, spiritual forces are set in motion that bring God's will to earth. God's will is accomplished in the spiritual realm and then revealed in the physical. From Daniel 10:12 we learn that spiritual forces were activated when Daniel set his heart toward God. "Then he [the angel] continued, 'Do not be afraid, Daniel. Since the first day that you set your mind to gain understanding and to humble yourself before your God, your words were heard, and I have come in response to them.'" The answer was not received in the physical realm for 21 days, although it began to come to earth the first day Daniel prayed. When the answer was revealed, the angel declared that it had come because of Daniel's words.

Let's examine Daniel's prayer. Read Daniel 10:1–14. Daniel needed an interpretation of a revelation or message that had come to him, so he began to pray and fast. Twenty-one days later a spiritual being appeared to Daniel to explain the message.

Did Daniel's prayer cause God to come up with an answer? No. When Daniel first began to pray, the answer was already prepared in heaven. God already knew the interpretation of the message. Did Daniel's prayer influence God's desires? No. When Daniel first began to pray, God already desired for Daniel to have the interpretation for which he was asking. Daniel's prayer simply released what God already had prepared and already desired to give him. Daniel's prayer brought God's will out of heaven onto earth.

The Power of God's Words

In the spiritual world, God's words are tangible. God talks about His own words as if they were alive.

> "So is my word that goes out from my mouth: It will not return to me empty, but will accomplish what I desire and achieve the purpose for which I sent it" (Isa. 55:11).

The book of Hebrews teaches us that God's words are indeed alive and active (see Heb. 4:12). My words, words initiated by my human nature, are not powerful and effective. God's words are powerful and effective.

God will put His word in our mouths. "'Now, I have put my words in your mouth'" (Jer. 1:9). Then He said, "'I am watching to see that my word is fulfilled'" (Jer. 1:12).

True prayer is God's words in your mouth. God is watching to see that His word is performed. He is not watching to see that our words are performed.

How does God put His words in your mouth? First God's desires must be in your heart. "'Out of the overflow of the heart the mouth speaks'" (Matt. 12:34). As God molds your heart to match His, the word of God that fills your heart is expressed in your words.

God teaches you and trains you. Eventually the work He is doing in your life, the truth He is teaching you, transforms your words. "The Sovereign Lord has given me an instructed tongue . . . . He wakens me morning by morning, wakens my ear to listen like one being taught" (Isa. 50:4). God teaches me and the result is an instructed tongue. "This is what we speak, not in words taught us by human wisdom, but in words taught by the Spirit, expressing spiritual truth in spiritual words" (1 Cor. 2:13). The spiritual truth revealed to us in our walk with God transforms our hearts. When our mouths speak out of the overflow of our hearts, our words are spiritual words, or words taught by the Spirit.

Our words, then, when they are words taught by the Spirit, are alive and tangible in the unseen world. Remember that Daniel's words activated God's will. Jesus gave us the authority to bind or loose on earth what has been so decreed in heaven. How would we do that? By our words, taught us by the Spirit and spoken in prayer. Jesus explained how to get God's will from heaven to the earth: He said, "Thy kingdom come. Thy will be done in earth, as it is in heaven." First our Spirit-taught words set in motion the spiritual forces that bring God's will to earth and overcome spiritual opposition (see Eph. 6:12 and then Eph. 3:10-11). Then our God-authored words create a bridge between the spiritual world and the physical world. Over this bridge, the will and the kingdom of God come to earth. What is so in heaven becomes so on earth.

Releasing God's Power for God's Purposes

God has given absolute authority to His Son. In Matthew 28:18 Jesus declares, "'All authority in heaven and on earth has been given to me.'" He has delegated that authority to us, deputized us to bring His will to earth through prayer. His authority is the basis of our prayer life. The proof of our delegated authority is His permission to use His name. The use of Jesus' name in prayer will be examined later. However, we understand that a person will not offer the use of his or her name to just anyone. This privilege is reserved for those who agree in purpose and method. The use of a person's name implies the full endorsement of the one whose name is used.

Jesus said in John 17:22: "'I have given them the glory that you gave me.'" Jesus has received all from the Father. Everything we are, we have received from Jesus. "All things are yours, . . . and you are of Christ, and Christ is of God" (1 Cor. 3:21,23). His purposes are our purposes. His life is our life. His authority is our authority. Through prayer we rule with Him, releasing the power of God to accomplish the will of God.

As God's heart is reproduced in us, the Holy Spirit directs our prayers so that we are praying for what God wants to give. Communication with God is true prayer only when its aim is to forbid or permit that which has already been forbidden or permitted in heaven. Through our prayers we rule with Christ from the right hand of God. We speak the will of God into the world by the authority of Christ.

Personal Prayer Experience

Release the kingdom of God and the will of God in every area of your life. Turn these Scripture verses into prayers.

My plans:	Proverbs 19:21
My personality:	John 12:24; Galatians 2:20
My worries and fears:	Isaiah 43:1-2
My family:	Ephesians 3:14-21; Jude 24-25
My past:	Philippians 3:13-14
My present:	Matthew 6:25-34
My future:	Jeremiah 29:11

THE AUTHOR OF PRAYER

Do you see how we have turned prayer upside down? We have spent our prayer energy trying to batter down the doors of heaven, get God's attention, and convince Him of the correctness of our point of view. This is not prayer! This is the

"God is in the process of answering even as we speak."
"Ask & we shall receive".

24   THE PRAYING LIFE

way of our human nature. This is speaking words taught by human wisdom, which have no influence with God or power in the spiritual world. In reality, we can't author prayer. Only God can author prayer.

From our human, limited perspectives, it may seem that we initiate prayer. We feel a need or experience a desire to pray. As a result, we pray. Actually, our felt needs or desires to pray are a response to God's initiative. Isaiah 65:24 says: "'Before they call I will answer; while they are still speaking I will hear.'" The answer is prepared before the request is made. God knew about your need before you did and prepared for it before you ever felt or experienced it.

Jeremiah 33:3 says: "'Call to me and I will answer you and tell you great and unsearchable things you do not know.'" God encourages us to call to Him. Why? So that we can tell Him things He otherwise would not know? No! He invites us to call to Him so that He can tell us things we otherwise would not know.

Prayer opens the way for God to act. Watchman Nee, in his book *Let Us Pray*, describes prayer like this: God's will is like a train and our prayers like a railroad track. A train has all the power necessary to travel from one location to another, but it can only travel to places where tracks have been laid. Our prayers fulfill God's conditions for the release of His will. God has the power to do whatever He wants, but has chosen to condition the demonstration of that power on our prayers.

In living a praying life, God's will is so exactly reproduced in us that it becomes our will. We find that when we pray the deepest desires of our hearts, we are stating His desires. These prayers are always answered. "'If you remain in me and my words remain in you, ask whatever you wish, and it will be given you'" (John 15:7), says Jesus. When our lives are dissolved in His and His Word shapes our prayers, all of our God-authored prayers are answered—no exceptions.

God's heart is the beginning point of prayer. Any request that does not begin with God is not true prayer. The content of our prayers is God's decision. Ezekiel 36:37 illustrates this. Here, through the prophet Ezekiel, God is foretelling the end of the days of Judah's judgment. In preceding verses He has described His good plan for Israel, which was not yet in effect. In verse 37 (NASB), He goes on to say: "'This also I will let the house of Israel ask Me to do for them.'" The house of Israel will ask for what God wants to give. God Himself will author their prayers. The answer was prepared before the request was made.

The Goal of Prayer: God's Glory

God wants to author our prayer lives in such a way that He will be glorified. Psalm 50:15 says: "'I will deliver you, and you will honor me.'" He wants our lives to become billboards upon which He can advertise Himself. He wants us to be living proof of Him. Through prayer we give Him permission to act in our lives in a way that will show His power and authority. Would you really want to be limited by your own imagination? First Corinthians 2:9 says that we have never experienced, nor could we imagine, what God has prepared for us. Ephesians 3:20 teaches the same truth: "Now to him who is able to do immeasurably more than all we ask or imagine." If we could command God, influencing Him to do our bidding, we would shortchange ourselves and miss the plan that exceeds our imaginations.

The story of Lazarus illustrates this principle (John 11). Mary and Martha sent an urgent message to Jesus as He was teaching in a nearby town, telling Him that their brother Lazarus was sick. The implication was that Jesus was to come right away so that Lazarus would not die. Jesus did not go immediately, but instead waited several days. In verses 21 and 32, both Mary and Martha state their firm belief that if Jesus had been there, Lazarus would not have died. They thought that expecting Jesus to heal Lazarus of a deadly illness was pushing the limits of His power. Now that Lazarus was dead, they reasoned, Jesus was too late.

Imagine their disillusionment and disappointment when Jesus failed to meet their expectations. Everything they understood about Jesus at that moment was threatened. What a crisis of faith they must have experienced.

Little did they suspect that Jesus would do more than heal Lazarus. He far exceeded their expectations when He raised

(Blackaby)

Lazarus from the dead. He enlarged their understanding of Him and His power. When God has access to our needs, He will always show us new things about Himself, leading us into a deeper walk with Him. We will learn to align ourselves with eternal realities and not have our faith sabotaged by time-bound, earthbound, shortsighted vision.

Personal Prayer Experience

Visualize God's presence in the person of Christ. Begin your prayertime by asking Him to set the agenda. Instead of jumping into your list of requests, ask Him: "Lord, what do you want to talk with me about?" Listen and respond.

Visualizing Jesus in conversation with you will help keep your mind focused as you listen.

THE PURPOSE OF PRAYER
REVIEW

1. Does prayer change God?

2. Will God work without an intercessor?

3. If not to change God, what is the true purpose of prayer?

4. God's goal in the praying life is to _____ His heart in us.

5. The main work in prayer is to _____ the _____ of God.

6. Although prayer does not change God's will, it does _____ God's will.

7. Why has God established prayer as the appointed way of accomplishing His will?

8. God wants us to be _____ in His kingdom, not _____.

9. What is the beginning point of prayer?

Answers: (1) no (review p. 9); (2) no (review p. 9); (3) to allow God to change us (review p. 9); (4) reproduce; (5) understand, heart; 6. activate; (7) God wants to live in relationship with us; (8) participants, observers; (9) the heart of God.

---

[1]When in the Scriptures it appears that God has changed His mind, the Spirit-inspired writer is using human terms to describe God. The theological term used for describing God in terms used to describe human emotions is *anthropopathism.*

4-11-95 \ 5:10 cim.

SECTION 2

THE PROCESS OF PRAYER

It is during the process of prayer that the praying person is brought to total submission to the Father. During the process of prayer, God weans our hearts from the things we so want and fastens them on Him. We start the process desiring something from Him and end it desiring only Him.

As I continued in the school of prayer, I recognized another misconception that was limiting my prayer life. I had assumed that prayer was composed of two parts, a request and an answer. I judged the strength of my prayer life by how many requests were granted, how many answers I could tally up in black and white. The instances when I could say, "I asked for . . . I got" were hits, other instances were misses. As I began to question why my prayer life, so defined, was hit-and-miss, God opened my eyes to a new understanding. Prayer is a process. Prayer is not summed up by request plus answer. It cannot be summed up in a simple two-part equation. Before the request is made, between the request and the answer, after the answer comes— all are part of the process of prayer. God has been at work, is at work, and will continue to be at work through our prayers in an ongoing process.

It is during the process of prayer that the praying person is brought to total submission to the Father. The lasting result of prayer does not lie in receiving the answer to a petition, but in submitting our lives to the process. Through the process of prayer, God fashions a heart like His. When we first begin to petition God concerning a need, our attention is focused on the answer for which we are waiting. During the process of prayer, God weans our hearts from the things we so want and fastens them on Him. We start the process desiring something from Him and finish the process desiring only Him. Our heart's cry becomes, "Whom have I in heaven but you? And being with you, I desire nothing on earth. My flesh and my heart may fail, but God is the strength of my heart and my portion forever. . . . But as for me, it is good to be near God" (Psalm 73:25-26,28).

The measure of a praying life, then, is not how many answers have been bestowed but how closely the praying person's heart matches the Father's. The result eventually will be more specific answers to prayer, but this will not be the measuring stick. If we welcome the prayer process and submit ourselves to it, we gain God Himself. We meet I AM face-to-face. We hear Him say, as He said to Abram, "'I am . . . your very great reward'" (Gen. 15:1). He builds into our very beings the understanding that He alone is worthy. Everything else pales before His presence. These lessons are woven into our lives during the process of prayer.

Personal Prayer Experience

Visualize Jesus on the throne of your life. Kneel before Him. Speak these words of love to Him: "As the deer pants for the streams of water, so my soul pants for you, O God" (Psalm 42:1).

As you kneel there, surrender yourself to Him—His timing, His purposes, His ways. Offer Him your impatience and your frustration with the process of prayer. Affirm your willingness to learn to desire only Him.

WAITING ON GOD

The most difficult part of the process of prayer is waiting on God. When we fail to recognize the waiting time as an indispensable ingredient of the prayer process, it becomes a time of discouragement and frustration. It is during the waiting times that many people drop out of the school of prayer. Not receiving their answers as expected, many conclude that prayer doesn't work, at least not for them.

While the waiting time is the most difficult part of the prayer process, it is also the most important. The waiting times give God the opportunity to redefine our desires and align our purpose and vision with His. While we wait, our spirits are being strengthened and refined. Remember Joseph. When he was a young man, God revealed His vision for Joseph. Joseph knew that he was ordained by God to be a great leader and that even his brothers would bow down to him. This was God's word, not Joseph's personal ambition. Yet Joseph waited for many years and endured many trials before God's promise took effect. Although Joseph was a man of upstanding moral character and pure devotion to the Lord, it was during this waiting period that God trained, strengthened, and prepared him.

Even though Joseph's waiting period appeared to have been engineered by men, it was really designed by God for His own purposes. Joseph summed his experience up like this: "'You intended to harm me, but God intended it for good to accomplish what is now being done'" (Gen. 50:20).

When we have petitioned and not received an answer, we may tend to grow fainthearted. Doubts may uproot us and leave us vulnerable. "He who doubts is like a wave of the sea, blown and tossed by the wind" (James 1:6). This is not how God intends the waiting period to be. When we respond correctly in submission and obedience, God provides the needed strength. Spiritual strength is one thing we will not have to wait for; it is there for the asking. "When I called, you answered me; you made me bold and stouthearted" (Psalm 138:3).

The opposite of one who doubts, one who is unstable in all he does, is one who endures, or perseveres. The person who perseveres is one whose roots grow deep. This person is not easily shaken or uprooted by circumstances. The maturity of a plant is not judged by its aboveground foliage, but by its underground root system.

How is this maturity, endurance, and steadfastness achieved? James describes the process like this: "Consider it pure joy, my brothers, whenever you face trials of many kinds, because you know that the testing of your faith develops perseverance. Perseverance must finish its work so that you may be mature and complete, not lacking anything" (James 1:2-4). Here, then, is the progression: *trials –> faith-tested and proven –> perseverance, or endurance –> maturity, or completeness.*

If God responded immediately to every petition, if He abolished the waiting period, our faith would never be exercised, endurance would never be developed, and we would never become mature and deeply rooted. God makes great use of His waiting periods.

Hannah: A Heart Like His

Consider Hannah, mother of Samuel. The account of Samuel's life begins with Hannah's yearning for a son. The true story of Samuel begins long before, in the heart of God. First Samuel 3:1 says, "In those days the word of the Lord was rare; there were not many visions." Under the old covenant, God spoke to His people through human messengers—priests or prophets. God entrusted His message to an individual and that individual passed it on to the people. From this verse we understand that God was displeased because He had no one whose heart was available to Him. He had no prophet through whom He could communicate with His people. In 1 Samuel 2:35, we discover that God has a plan to remedy this situation. "'I will raise up for myself a faithful priest, who will do according to what is in my heart and mind.'" Before Hannah began to long for a son, God was already longing for a prophet.

In the first chapter of 1 Samuel, the Scriptures say of Hannah, "The Lord had closed her womb." This seems a cruel, heartless act of a merciless God unless we view the story from beginning to end; unless we see the process through which God guided Hannah. Before Hannah prayed, God was already at work laying the groundwork for His prophet; while Hannah was praying, God was at work preparing Hannah's life for His answer; and after Hannah's prayer had been answered, God was at work among His people through His prophet Samuel, the answer to Hannah's petition.

Hannah, we learn, was in great emotional pain because of her barrenness. She wept and would not eat. Her lack of children was a public disgrace. She suffered the taunting of Penninah, her husband's other wife. From a human, one-dimensional perspective, it seemed that God had forgotten Hannah. Hannah could not get God to move on her behalf.

The turning point in this story comes in 1 Samuel 1:11. Hannah prays this prayer: "'O Lord Almighty, if you will only look upon your servant's misery and remember me, and not forget your servant but give her a son, then I will give him to the Lord for all the days of his life, and no razor will ever be used on his head.'" (The vow that a razor would never touch his head referred to the practice of the Nazirite sect, refusing to cut their hair lest a man-made tool profane this God-given growth. Although Samuel was never a Nazirite, this further indicates that Hannah would consecrate her son totally to God.) Following this prayer, Hannah conceived and bore her long-awaited son, Samuel.

Why does this prayer seem to touch the heart of God, when her many prayers before seemed not to? The difference lies not in the prayer, but in the woman. From the beginning of her ordeal, Hannah was ready to be the mother of a son. Now she is ready to be the mother of a prophet. God has done His mighty work. God's heart and Hannah's heart are a perfect match. The miracle is not in the physical manifestation of the glory of God when barren Hannah bore a son; the miracle is in the heart of Hannah, now forever stamped with the character of God.

The answer to Hannah's petition is not the end of God's work, but the beginning. Now Hannah has her son and God has His prophet. "The boy Samuel grew up in the presence of the Lord" (1 Sam. 2:21). Samuel became a great intercessor for the nation of Israel. He became the fulfillment of God's vision of a faithful priest. "Throughout Samuel's lifetime, the hand of the Lord was against the Philistines" (1 Sam. 7:13). God's hand was against the enemies of Israel, not all the days that there was a warrior on the battlefield, but all the days there was a warrior in the prayer closet.

Lazarus: God's Bigger Agenda

Look again at the story of Lazarus in John 11. Lazarus and his sisters were dear friends of Jesus. In fact, it was Mary who had anointed Jesus' feet with ointment and wiped them with her hair. Since they were such close friends, Mary and Martha sent a message to Jesus. Their message was simple and indicated their absolute faith in Jesus to respond to their needs. "'Lord, the one you love is sick.'" The story continues like this:

> Jesus loved Martha and her sister and Lazarus. Yet when he
> heard that Lazarus was sick, . . .

How would you finish that sentence? I would finish it this way: Jesus loved Martha and Mary and Lazarus, so when Jesus heard that Lazarus was sick, He dropped everything and hurried to Bethany. Those would be my words, taught by human wisdom. But the Holy Spirit finishes the sentence differently.

> Jesus loved Martha and her sister and Lazarus. Yet when he
> heard that Lazarus was sick, he stayed where he was two
> more days (John 11:5-6).

Does that defy human understanding? He loved them so much that He allowed time to elapse before responding to their request. He didn't wait a few days because He was distracted, or didn't hear their request, or didn't care. He waited because He loved them so much.

Jesus said another strange thing to His disciples. "'Lazarus is dead, and for your sake I am glad I was not there, so that you may believe'" (John 11:14-15). Jesus' apparent delay was deliberate, loving, and purposeful. Jesus said that the delay was more profitable for His disciples than an immediate answer would have been.

Let's stop and put this whole story into its eternal context. Mary and Martha had a need: their brother was sick and dying. Their need was urgent: Lazarus had only days to live. Mary's and Martha's immediate, urgent need was the focus of their prayer. Their prayer would be answered if Jesus had come immediately and healed Lazarus.

Jesus never acted on His own initiative, but acted in obedience to the Father. God loved Lazarus. He knew that Lazarus was sick and dying. He wanted to heal Lazarus. But God wanted to do more than just heal Lazarus. God had a bigger agenda, not a different agenda.

If Jesus had met Mary's and Martha's expectations, if He had come quickly and healed Lazarus, who would have seen God's glory? Mary, Martha, Lazarus, and the disciples. Would they have learned anything new about Jesus? No.

They already knew Jesus had the power to heal.

Since Jesus delayed, "many Jews had come to Martha and Mary to comfort them in the loss of their brother" (John 11:19). He waited until Lazarus had been dead for four days. Then, with everyone watching, Jesus displayed the power of God over death. He taught the truth: "'I am the resurrection and the life. He who believes in me will live, even though he dies'" (John 11:25). He backed up His words with a physical display that authenticated His claim. He raised Lazarus from the dead. "Therefore many of the Jews who had come to visit Mary, and had seen what Jesus did, put their faith in him" (John 11:45). Jesus used their need to stretch their faith and to bring many to new faith in Him. He did more than they could ask or imagine, and it required a waiting period.

God Schedules Waiting Periods

In the praying life, God schedules waiting periods. Out of His loving-kindness and tender mercy, He allows His children to wait. These periods when God seems to be deaf to our most fervent cries, the truth is He is in the process of answering. God is always at work. "He who watches over you will not slumber" (Psalm 121:3). He had begun to answer before we called. He will use this time to multiply our strength (Isa. 40:31), to put iron in our souls. He will purify our faith so that our trust is in Him alone. He will fasten our hearts on Him.

God will use these periods to teach about the wisdom of His timing. We will learn to look at time like our Father does. He works in fulfilled time, not elapsed time. He doesn't measure time by a calendar, but by eternity. "'The time is fulfilled, and the kingdom of God is at hand'" (Mark 1:15 NASB). Fulfilled time is not defined by the passing of days, but by the readiness of the circumstances. When the time is ripe, when every piece is in place, God will act. His concern is not time, but timing. In the course of waiting on God, we will learn to pray in the spirit of the psalmist: "But as for me, my prayer is to thee, O Lord. At an acceptable time, O God, in the abundance of thy steadfast love answer me" (Psalm 69:13 RSV).

Personal Prayer Experience

What are you waiting for? What has God been accomplishing in you while you wait? Write out your thoughts.

Write out a statement of your surrender to God's timing and purposes. Sign and date it.

Pray this prayer: "But as for me, my prayer is to Thee, O Lord. At an acceptable time, O God, in the abundance of thy steadfast love answer me" (Psalm 69:13 RSV).

4-13-95

1:∞ a.m.

HEARING FROM GOD

4-15-95 2:∞ am

Hearing from God is the central work of prayer. During the prayer process, God is attuning our ears to His voice. Jesus said, "'My sheep listen to my voice . . . and they follow me'" (John 10:27). As a sheep learns to recognize the voice of its shepherd, so we learn to recognize our Shepherd's voice. Through the steady discipline of prayer, He trains us to distinguish between His voice and the voices of strangers. The ability to hear and respond to Him elevates us to a new level of relationship. Jesus told His disciples, "'I no longer call you servants, because a servant does not know his master's business. Instead, I have called you friends, for everything that I learned from my Father I have made known to you'" (John 15:15). The difference between being a slave and being a friend, Jesus explained, is the ability to hear from Him and know His heart.

We must be able to hear from God because He alone is the

source of true prayer. His desires are poured into our hearts so that they become our desires and are expressed through our prayers—this is the goal of the praying life. "Behold, I will pour out my thoughts to you; I will make my words known to you" (Prov. 1:23 RSV). He will be generous in His revelation. He will pour out His thoughts. In true prayer our minds come into contact with the mind of God. His thoughts are reproduced in us so that we think the very thoughts of God. God's thoughts expressed through our words, or God's words in our mouths, is prayer.

The Scriptures are filled with invitations to listen to God. "Whether you turn to the right or to the left, your ears will hear a voice behind you, saying, 'This is the way; walk in it'" (Isa. 30:21). "'I will instruct you and teach you in the way you should go'" (Psalm 32:8). "'Today, if you hear his voice, do not harden your hearts'" (Heb. 4:7). When we are instructed to hear His voice, we are also admonished to respond. He speaks, not to inform, but to transform.

God's revelation of Himself is spoken. His words express His character and carry His authority. His words are His pledge. He spoke the world into existence. "God said . . . and it was so" is the story of creation. In the ultimate communication, God's Word became flesh and dwelt among us. That Word, Jesus, the embodiment of all God's words, is now the channel of God's communication with His people. "In the past God spoke to our forefathers through the prophets at many times and in various ways, but in these last days he has spoken to us by His Son" (Heb. 1:1-2). God's communication, while the imperfect old covenant was in effect, came in small portions and from various sources. It was always a partial revelation. But now, we who are heirs under the new, ever-lasting covenant, have His complete revelation from one source—Jesus Christ, "in whom are hidden all the treasures of wisdom and knowledge" (Col. 2:3). "No man has seen God at any time; the only begotten God, who is in the bosom of the Father, He has explained Him" (John 1:18 NASB).

God has now revealed Himself. The human Jesus was the visible image of the invisible God. He continues to reveal God within us through the Holy Spirit.

Three in One

Let me try to illustrate the oneness of the Father, the Son, and the Spirit in Their communication to you. I am not the body I live in. The real me is made up of my feelings, experiences, and perceptions which form the basis of my thoughts. My thoughts are with me and my thoughts are me. My thoughts originate in me and you cannot separate me from my thoughts—they are one and the same. However, no one will know my thoughts, or know me, unless I express my thoughts in words. My words are my thoughts expressed audibly.

My words and my thoughts are exactly the same.

My words are the exact representation of my thoughts.

The power that gives voice to my thoughts is my breath. My breath passing over my vocal chords produces my voice to speak my words. I am the originator of my thoughts, my words are the expression of my thoughts, and my breath is the power that makes my words audible. This is my communication. There is no need to separate thoughts, words, and breath because they are all the same action. Communication is not effective except when all three components are operating. My thoughts, my words, and my breath are three in one.

God's thoughts are precious to you and so vast that they outnumber the grains of sand (see Psalm 139:17-18). Yet God's wonderful thoughts cannot affect your life unless you know them. God must put His thoughts into words. "In the beginning was the Word, and the Word was with God, and the Word was God. . . . The Word became flesh and lived for a while among us. . . . No one has ever seen God, but God the only Son, who is at the Father's side, has made Him known. . . . The Son is . . . the exact representation of His being" (John 1:1,14,18; Heb. 1:3). Just as my words and my thoughts are the same, so Jesus (the Word) and the Father (the Divine Thinker) are the same.

Jesus is God. He is the complete and exact expression of God. He is the truth. Jesus is communicated to you by the Spirit, the Breath of God. "'He [the Holy Spirit] will bring glory to me [Jesus] by taking from what is mine and making it known to you. All that belongs to the Father is mine. That is why I said the Spirit will take from what is mine and make it known to you'" (John 16:14). The Father, the Son, and the Holy Spirit are equal and work in perfect harmony to reveal Themselves to you. We must learn to listen for the God-breathed word that is the content of true prayer.

Know God By Revelation

God has made it clear that He cannot be fully known from any outside source. That was the old covenant way. Now we have "a better covenant, which was established upon better promises" (Heb. 8:6 KJV). The new arrangement changes the source of communication from outside to inside.

> "'The time is coming, declares the Lord, when I will make a new covenant with the house of Israel and with the house of Judah. It will not be like the covenant I made with their fore-fathers. . . . I will put my laws in their minds and write them on their hearts. I will be their God, and they will be my people. No longer will a man teach his neighbor, or a man his brother, saying, "Know the Lord," because they will all know me, from the least of them to the greatest'" (Heb. 8:8-11). Jer. 31: 31-34

Do you see how the writer of Hebrews contrasts the two covenants? In the first, God's words were outside, guiding; in the second, God's word is inside, transforming.

God reveals Himself to you from within. He speaks directly to you by means of revelation, the direct action of God on your soul.

"However, as it is written, 'No eye has seen, no ear has heard, no mind has conceived what God has prepared for those who love Him,' but God has revealed it to us by his Spirit" (1 Cor. 2:9-10). Again, God cannot be known by using our physical senses or human imaginations. We cannot even imagine all that God has prepared for us. Yet that which cannot be known by hearing or seeing or reflecting can be known by revelation—by hearing with spiritual ears.

Information comes from outside sources. Revelation comes from within. Information is filtered through the mind. The mind cannot understand the things of the Spirit because they are spiritually discerned. Spiritual truth is not explained; it is revealed.

I keep asking that the God of our Lord Jesus Christ, the glorious Father, may give you the Spirit of wisdom and revelation,
so that you may know him better (Eph. 1:17).

We have not stopped praying for you and asking God to fill
you with the knowledge of his will through all spiritual wisdom and understanding (Col. 1:9).

Because God Himself indwells you, all spiritual truth is
within you. Since Jesus is the truth and He indwells you,
truth is within you. The Father, the Son, and the Holy Spirit
have made Their home in you. Jesus said of those who would
believe His words, "'We will come to him and make our
home with him'" (John 14:23). He prayed in John 17:23, "'I in
them and you in me.'" Ephesians says that we are with Him
where He is—at God's right hand. The Trinity is inseparable.
They are Three in One.

All of God lives in your spirit: the thoughts, the word, and
the voice. All truth lives in your spirit.

As for you, the anointing you received from him remains in
you, and you do not need anyone to teach you. But as his
anointing teaches you about all things and as that anointing is
real, not counterfeit—just as it has taught you, remain in him"
(1 John 2:27).

"'No longer will a man teach his neighbor, or a man his
brother, saying, "Know the Lord," because they will all know
me, from the least of them to the greatest'" (Heb. 8:11).

Why, then, do we not understand all truth? Because our
minds, part of our human nature and in need of the Spirit's
renewal, do not know all truth.

When we seek to know God by information, we fill our
minds with knowledge about God and hope it will seep into
our spirits. But God cannot be known by information alone.
Spiritual truth is spiritually discerned, or known, first in the
spirit. Instead of truth coming through the mind to the spirit,
truth comes from the spirit to the mind.

The following illustrations will help you see the difference
between information and revelation. Look at illustration A.

ILLUSTRATION A

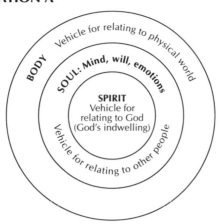

Human beings have a body through which to relate to or interact with the physical world; a soul (Greek: *psuche*), or personality (mind, will, and emotions) through which to interact with each other; and a spirit (Greek: *pneuma*), through which to relate to God. God indwells your spirit and expresses Himself through your personality and through your body.

Look at illustration B.

ILLUSTRATION B

"'I will put my laws in their minds and write them on their hearts. I will be their God, and they will be my people. No longer will a man teach his neighbor, or a man his brother, saying, "Know the Lord," because they will all know me, from the least of them to the greatest'" (Heb. 8:10-11).

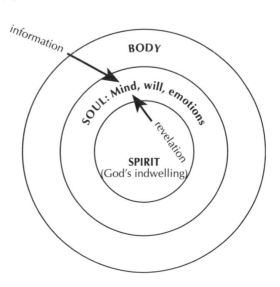

Information comes from outside. Information must make its way through several barriers in order to reach your understanding. It has to be filtered through layers of perceptions, preconceived ideas, opinions, judgments, etc. Have you ever said something to someone and he or she has misinterpreted your meaning? What the person understood was not what you said. By the time it reached the other person's understanding, it was completely distorted.

This is why information is an inadequate source of knowledge about God. The old covenant was based on information about God. God spoke to His people using outside sources. That's why He said that the new covenant will not be like the old covenant. Information hardens into ritual and fear and inflexibility. It is secondhand knowledge. God wants you to have direct knowledge—revelation. He wants to speak from within straight into your understanding. He Himself will write His laws on your heart and on your mind.

God Himself Unveils Truth

The word *revelation* means "unveiling" or "uncovering." Our human nature, or flesh, is symbolized by the veil in the Temple (Heb. 10:20 [NASB]: "the veil, that is, His flesh") that kept people outside the Holy of Holies, or presence of God (Heb. 9:3). When Moses met God face-to-face, the skin of Moses' face shone with the presence of God. Moses had to put a veil over his face. Again, the presence of God was hidden behind a veil.

People who are without Jesus are "darkened in their understanding" (Eph. 4:18). Second Corinthians says that there is a veil over the understanding, or mind, of anyone who has not turned to the Lord (read 2 Cor. 3:12-16 in the *Amplified Bible*). "But whenever anyone turns to the Lord, the veil is taken away" (2 Cor. 3:16 NIV).

God lifts the veil over your mind or understanding. He "unveils" the Truth in your spirit to your mind. He does not unveil all truth at once. This unveiling happens progressively as we walk with Him.

Information or Revelation?

First Corinthians 2:9-16 sums up the contrast between information and revelation. "'No eye has seen, no ear has heard, no mind has conceived what God has prepared for those who love him'" (v. 9).

"But God has revealed it to us by his Spirit. The Spirit searches all things, even the deep things of God." What we cannot know by human wisdom, God has shown us by means of His Spirit. Where is His Spirit? His Spirit indwells you.

"For who among men knows the thoughts of a man except the man's spirit within him?" In other words, no one knows you but you. No one will ever know your innermost thoughts unless you reveal them. Another person cannot reveal your thoughts because no other person knows your thoughts.

"In the same way no one knows the thoughts of God except the Spirit of God." Just like no one knows you but you, no one knows God but God. No one but God can reveal the deep things of God. "We have not received the spirit of the world but the Spirit who is from God, that we may understand what God has freely given us." God has revealed Himself. He has injected Himself into us and will think His thoughts through our minds, express His emotions through our emotions, and speak His desires through our words. He wants us to understand what He has freely given us, so He has revealed Himself through His indwelling presence.

Once we understand what God has given us, what are we to do with this revelation? We are to speak it. "This is what we speak, not in words taught us by human wisdom but in words taught by the Spirit, expressing spiritual truths in spiritual words." God's words, taught us by the Spirit, accomplish God's purposes. Those words succeed in the matter for which He sends them. Why? Because they are God's very own words spoken in prayer by us.

"The man without the Spirit does not accept the things that come from the Spirit of God, for they are foolishness to him, and he cannot understand them, because they are spiritually discerned." The deep things of God are understood in the spirit and revealed to the mind. They cannot be filtered through the mind from outside sources. The person without the Spirit cannot understand spiritual truths because they are coming to him or her as information.

"The spiritual man makes judgments about all things, but he himself is not subject to any man's judgment: 'For who has known the mind of the Lord that he may instruct him?' But we have the mind of Christ." Do you see the contrast? The mind of Christ is not to instruct God, but to receive instruction from Him. Jesus' earthly life taught us that He was always listening for God's instruction. "'I tell you the truth, the Son can do nothing by himself; he can do only what he sees his Father doing, because whatever the Father does the Son also does'" (John 5:19). "'Don't you believe that I am in the Father, and that the Father is in me? The words I say to you are not just my own. Rather, it is the Father, living in me, who is doing his work'" (John 14:10). "'These words you hear are not my own; they belong to the Father who sent me'" (John 14:24).

We can't instruct God. We only see a poor reflection, as in an imperfect mirror (see 1 Cor. 13:12). "As you do not know the path of the wind, or how the body is formed in a mother's womb, so you cannot understand the work of God, the Maker of all things" (Eccl. 11:5). "How unsearchable his judgments, and his paths beyond tracing out!" (Rom. 11:33). You can only know God as He graciously reveals Himself to you. You cannot instruct Him, but only respond to His revelation.

The more we learn to walk in the Spirit and put no confidence in the flesh, the more revelation we receive; the more "the God of our Lord Jesus Christ, the glorious Father, may give to you the Spirit of wisdom and of revelation, so that you may know Him better" (Eph. 1:17), the more you will be filled "with the knowledge of his will through all spiritual wisdom and understanding" (Col. 1:9). It will become true of you as was true of the disciples: "Then He opened their minds so they could understand the Scriptures" (Luke 24:45).

God has placed the gifts of teaching, preaching, and prophecy in the body because they are His tools for unveiling truth. The faithful practice of these gifts is one way that God brings revelation. However, remember this: If through the teaching or preaching of a person you come to understand spiritual truth, that is not because the person is a good teacher or preacher or writer or singer, but because God Himself is lifting the veil over your understanding. You did not receive spiritual understanding from a person, but from God, Whose tools are sometimes people.

Hear God By the Spirit

The capacity to hear God's voice is given to us by Him. "Thou hast given me an open ear" (Psalm 40:6 RSV). God gives spiritual ears just as He gives physical ears. While physical ears may be defective, spiritual ears never are. "He . . . wakens my ear to listen like one being taught. The Sovereign Lord has opened my ears" (Isa. 50:4-5).

Through the ages, those who have heard and responded to God's voice have been changed by it. Abram was an idol worshiper living comfortably in Ur of the Chaldeans (Josh. 24:2). But God spoke. And Abram, idol worshiper, became Abraham, friend of God. He followed the Voice that spoke clearly in his inmost being and the eternal redemptive plan was set in motion. Impetuous, emotional Simon received God's revelation that Jesus was the Christ. Jesus began that day to call him Peter, the rock, not based on who he was, but who he would become as a result of hearing God. Saul heard Jesus on the Damascus Road. Saul, persecutor of the church, became Paul, planter and nurturer of churches.

How do we hear God? Haven't many outrageous things been done and declared under the guise of having heard God? Isn't it arrogant to think that I could have a direct revelation from God Almighty?

First of all, we must believe that God wants us to hear Him and that He has provided the way. Second, we must let God purify our hearts to want only Him. Third, we must focus our attention on Him by engaging in spiritual disciplines. We must come to Him without preconceived ideas of what He will say. We must be planted in the body of Christ. We must give Him time. Wait on the Lord.

God will speak most often and most clearly through His Word. To hear Him we must be engaged in the discipline of reading God's Word every day. He will take His Word and speak directly and personally to you. His truth will be unveiled regarding specific acts of obedience, words of love and encouragement, or wisdom in certain situations. Sometimes His communication will not be formed in words, but will be an understanding or knowledge that could be from no other source. At times you will find God's communication simply poured through you as you pray. If we listen, we will hear Him. If we are allowing Him to do His purifying work in our hearts, we will know His voice. God's still, small voice will drown out all other voices . . . in an uncluttered heart.

Through the Holy Spirit, Jesus can speak more effectively within us than He could speak to His disciples when He was with them physically. Through our spiritual senses, He speaks directly into our understanding. When Jesus told His disciples that He would be leaving them to return to the Father, they were sorrowful. Jesus explained to them that His life within them would be better than having His physical presence with them.

> "'But I tell you the truth: it is for your good that I am going away. Unless I go away, the Counselor will not come to you; but if I go, I will send him to you. . . . But when he, the Spirit of truth, comes, he will guide you into all truth. He will not speak on his own; he will speak only what he hears, and he will tell you what is yet to come'" (John 16:7,13).

You can hear Jesus today with your spiritual ears. The disciples heard Him with their physical ears. You have more immediate access to Him and more intimate knowledge of Him and more direct experience of Him than those 12 men did while they knew Him on earth. God, Jesus, the Holy Spirit, with one voice, are speaking to you now.

Hearing from God is an integral part of the prayer process. What is our confidence before Him? "This is the assurance we have in approaching God: that if we ask anything according to his will, he hears us. And if we know that he hears us— whatever we ask—we know that we have what we asked of him" (1 John 5:14-15). We must be able to hear from God so that we can come confidently before Him, asking for what He longs to give. Until and unless He gives more specific guidance, "Thy kingdom come. Thy will be done" is the prayer that releases God's will.

This is not a passive, uninvolved, arm's-length prayer. This prayer actively and deliberately establishes the kingdom and the will of God in a situation. "Thy kingdom come. Thy will be done" brings the spiritual world to bear on the physical world. This prayer reaches into heaven to pull God's kingdom onto the earth.

Personal Prayer Experience

Arrange an extended time of silence and solitude. Listen to God and respond. Visualize His presence to help you keep your mind focused without feeling the need to fill up silence with words. Wait on the Lord"!   2:43

SEEKING AFTER GOD

The reward of a search is finding that which is sought. If you seek a lost treasure, your search will be rewarded by finding the very treasure you were seeking. God "rewards those who earnestly seek him" (Heb. 11:6). The certain reward for seeking God is finding Him. "'You will seek me and find me when you seek me with all your heart'" (Jer. 29:13).

Promise

The secret to finding God is seeking Him. He Himself must be the focal point of our search, not blessings by way of Him, but Him. In finding Him, we find everything.

We must seek Him wholeheartedly. God invites us to pray, "Give me an undivided heart, that I may fear your name" (Psalm 86:11). He invites us to ask for what He is ready and able to give. In the book of James, the double-minded are called upon to purify their hearts. A pure heart, then, is an undivided heart.

As God lovingly leads us through the prayer process, He invites us to seek Him and find Him. The irony of seeking God is to find that what seems like initiative is really a response. "Thou hast said, 'Seek ye my face.' My heart says to Thee, 'Thy face, O Lord, do I seek'" (Psalm 27:8 RSV). In the course of seeking Him, we find that He is seeking us (John 4:23). This dual search is part of the process of learning to pray.

As always, God will take full responsibility for bringing about that which He requires. He requires a heart set on Him. He alone can supply such a heart. "I will give them a heart to know me, that I am the Lord'" (Jer. 24:7).

How do we seek God? We seek Him by engaging in spiritual disciplines. The outward disciplines of the spiritual life will not reveal God. However, as we engage in those disciplines, God will reveal Himself. To seek means to inquire diligently, to search carefully. "If you seek her as silver, and search for her as for hidden treasures; then you will discern the fear of the Lord, and discover the knowledge of God" (Prov. 2:4-5 NASB). "'Seek and you will find'" (Matt. 7:7).

God's Word

Through a consistent daily intake of God's word, God will reveal His heart and mold our prayers. God's word nourishes our spirits, just as food nourishes our bodies. Jesus compared God's word to food when He said, "Man does not live on bread alone, but on every word that comes from the mouth of God" (Matt. 4:4). The prophet Jeremiah said, "When your words came, I ate them; they were my joy and my heart's delight" (Jer. 15:16). God's words energized and nourished Jeremiah's spirit.

Physically, when you eat food, the nutrients from that food are absorbed into your bloodstream to be deposited in your cells. How do the right nutrients reach the right cells? How does calcium get to your bone cells? How does protein get to your muscle cells? Why don't the nutrients get deposited in the wrong cells? Our food all enters our bodies the same way, and yet the specific nutrients get to the specific cells. How does that occur?

Every cell has its own specifically designed receptacles (receptor sites) that draw out of your bloodstream exactly the nutrients needed to nourish that cell. Amazing! You have billions and billions of cells in your body, each drawing nutrients out of your bloodstream. This complicated and sophisticated process happens without your effort. You don't even have to know what happens or how it happens for it to happen. You don't have to feel it happening. You eat the food and your digestive system applies it to your body. The nutrients in your food literally come to life in your body.

Nourishing your spirit is the same way. You feast on God's word, and God Himself will apply it to your life. God's word is alive and active. It is not living and active written on paper and bound in a book. It is given life by the Holy Spirit when it is in your life. It comes to life in you as it comes in contact with your faith (see Heb. 4:2). When you read God's Word, God unveils truth to your understanding. He takes responsibility for applying His word within you. He opens your mind to understand the Scriptures.

What would happen if you did not eat the foods that contain the nutrients your cells need? Your cells would have no nutrients to draw. Your bloodstream only has available the nutrients you have ingested. If you don't take in the word of God, your spirit has no nourishment to draw from. We must look for every possible way to ingest His word. We will not hear God's specific guidance through His Word by spasmodic, occasional Bible reading. The effect of the Scriptures is cumulative.

We will not hear Him clearly if we look for His communication only at certain times for certain circumstances. God speaks to us through His Word as part of the prayer process, one aspect of a praying life. We must approach our Bible study listening for Him, whatever He would say, not listening for an instant solution to our perceived problems. Many times God's communication helps us redefine our problems. Our ideas of God, our definitions of God, cloud our vision and hide God from us. Too often we come to Him expecting Him to validate our decisions, and so miss Him altogether. In listening for God, we must approach Him without preconceived notions of what He will say. We must come with open ears.

If we ask Him for an undivided heart and ask Him to reveal Himself through His Word, He will show us what to pray. Why will He show us what to pray? So that we can approach Him confidently; so that we can be the channels of His will; so that we can stand in the gap between heaven and earth.

Solitude and Silence

To seek God, we must build into our lives the discipline of solitude and silence. We must allow God to allure us into the wilderness where He can speak tenderly to us (Hos. 2:14). Although prayer is continuous, an ongoing interchange of love between the Father and His child, there must be scheduled times when all of our attention is directed toward God. Early morning is the best time for this. We are refreshed from a night of sleep, the day has not yet crowded in on us, the rest of the world is asleep, and we are alone. Jesus left us this example in His earthly life: "Very early in the morning, while it was still dark, Jesus got up, left the house and went off to a solitary place, where he prayed" (Mark 1:35). We must be able to withdraw for a while from the fevered pace of our lives, from the noise and incessant demands, to listen for the still, small voice within.

We need to deliberately seek silence. We need to turn off the electronic noises that fill our lives. We need to escape the mind-set that compels us to fill up the silence with televisions and telephones and music. We must remember, as the prophet Elijah learned, that God's usually is not the loudest or most strident voice. His voice is not to be heard in the great and strong wind, nor in the earthquake, nor in the fire. His voice is a gentle blowing in your innermost being (see 1 Kings 19:11-13). His voice is not hard to hear . . . if you're listening.

Fasting

Another spiritual discipline to be incorporated into our lives is the discipline of fasting. Fasting is not a way to influence, impress, or manipulate God. It is not a hunger strike designed to convince God to release that which He has, up to now, held back. Fasting is a tangible way to let go of that which ties us to our physical world, food, in order to receive all our sustenance from the spiritual world. For a short time, we deprive our physical appetites to feed our spiritual appetites. During a fast, spiritual cravings take priority over physical cravings. "'I have food to eat that you know nothing about. . . . My food . . . is to do the will of him who sent me and to finish his work'" (John 4:32,34). Fasting is more than going without food. During a fast, we replace eating with prayer, Bible study, and listening to God.

Fasting is not a last-ditch effort to get through to God. Instead, it sharpens our spiritual senses so that God can get through to us. Second Chronicles 20 tells the story of a fast. Jehoshaphat, king of Judah, received word that a great multitude was coming against him from beyond the sea. Verse 3 states that Jehoshaphat "resolved to inquire of the Lord, and he proclaimed a fast for all Judah." As a part of the process of seeking God, Jehoshaphat proclaimed a fast. In verses 6-12, Jehoshaphat reiterated the promises of God. He prayed God's expressed will. He knew what God wanted to do, but not how He wanted to do it. Verse 12 expresses the attitude of a fast. "'We have no power to face this vast army that is attacking us. We do not know what to do, but our eyes are upon Thee.'" While the people of Judah were fasting and standing before the Lord, God revealed what they were to do. "You will not have to fight this battle. Take your positions; stand firm and see the deliverance the Lord will give you, O Judah and Jerusalem" (v. 17).

Jehoshaphat still did not know how God would fulfill His promises, but he knew what action he was to take. Jehoshaphat knew the outcome, but not the details. God usually reveals His will one step at a time. When the people responded in obedience to God's command, God's power was released on their behalf. Their enemies destroyed one another. As a result of turning their attention to seek the Lord and proclaiming a fast, they heard God.

Jesus fasted to prepare Himself for His battle with Satan. He was led by the Spirit into the wilderness for the express purpose of being tempted by the devil (Matt. 4:1-2). In preparation, He fasted. His body was weakened, but His spirit was mighty.

It was while the leaders of the early church were worshiping and fasting that the Holy Spirit spoke and told them to send out Saul and Barnabas. They prayed and fasted more before laying hands on them and sending them out (Acts 13:2-3).

Jesus fasted during His earthly life and left explicit instructions about fasting. In Matthew 6:16-18, He taught His disciples that fasting was between each individual and the Father. "Your Father, who sees what is done in secret, will reward you" (Matt. 6:8).[1] What will be the reward of fasting? The presence of God Himself. He is a rewarder of those who seek Him. "Surely you have granted him eternal blessings and made him glad with joy of your presence" (Psalm 21:6). The presence of God is its own reward.

Fellowship

Finally, we must be involved in the discipline of fellowship with believers. We must be an active part of a local church. Christ expresses Himself in His fullness through His body (Eph. 1:23). Within the context of the body of Christ, we attain our maturity and the full knowledge of God (Eph. 4:13). The proper working of each individual part causes the growth of the body (Eph. 4:16). The Christian who separates himself or herself from the body cannot know God fully and cannot hear Him clearly.

In learning that prayer is an ongoing process, a walk, a relationship, I learned to see the work of God as continuous. I can no longer separate my life into segments: "God answered this prayer, but not this one." God's work has no clearly defined beginning and ending points. One experience blends into the next, a never-ending process of maturing. The Holy Spirit builds understanding brick by brick. Would I, then, surrender myself to God, allowing Him to accomplish His purpose, in His time, in His way? Would I allow Him to determine my course and direct my path? Would I let Him, through the process of prayer, re-create His heart in me?

Personal Prayer Experience

Have you been seeking God? Have you been rewarded with His presence? Take time now, in the presence of God, to set your heart on Him. Write Him a letter.

THE PROCESS OF PRAYER
REVIEW

1. During the process of prayer, God _____ our Pg. 31 hearts from the thing we so want and _____ them on Him.

2. Why does God schedule waiting periods? Pg. 37

3. God's concern is not time, but _____. Pg. 37

4. Jesus does not call us slaves, but instead calls us friends, Pg. 38 because_____

   _____

   _____

5. God's _____ expressed through our _____ is Pg. 39 prayer.

6. God communicates to us from _____, not by out- Pg. 41 side sources.

7. What is the difference between revelation and information?

pg. 41

8. We seek God by engaging in _____.

Pg. 50

Answers: (1) weans, fastens; (2) to align our vision and desires with His; (3) timing; (4) a slave doesn't know what his
master is doing, but Jesus makes known to us everything the
Father makes known to Him; (5) desires, words; (6) within;
(7) information comes from outside sources, revelation comes
from God within; (8) spiritual disciplines.

------

¹This passage is not to be interpreted to mean that a prayer request that
has not been granted will be granted if the petitioner fasts.

4-17-95
2:45- 3:45

SECTION 3

THE PROMISE OF PRAYER

The promise of prayer is a transformed heart. Once God has taught us and changed us through the prayer process, every prayer promise is ours. Our hearts belong to Him alone and He can plant in them His divine desires and make them ours.

The promise of prayer is a transformed heart. Through the ongoing discipline of prayer, we are brought into intimate contact with God. As we continually behold His glory, we are changed into His image. Our inner beings begin to reflect Him. As He has constant access to us, He re-aligns our vision, re-creates our desires, reproduces His heart. The promise of prayer is that He will grant us our heart's desires and not withhold the requests of our lips. The promise of prayer is the result of the process of prayer. Once God has taught us and changed us through the prayer process, every prayer promise is ours. Our hearts belong to Him alone and He can plant in them His divine desires and make them ours. Enthroned in our lives, He can channel His good plans into the world through our prayers. By allowing our lives to be absorbed in His, we can bit by bit be freed of our shortsighted desires and participate in eternity.

The all-encompassing promise "'Ask whatever you wish, and it will be given you'" (John 15:7) is directed toward those who abide in Him and who allow His words to abide in them. That person's desires are God-shaped. The prayer promises in the Scriptures must be put into context. They are not blank checks. Every prayer promise is linked to a spiritual require-ment. Prayer is more than the words we speak. Our relation-ship as child to Father is what makes our words prayer.

Suppose you ordered a meal at a restaurant. When the waitress brought your meal, suppose she said, "That looks delicious! I think I'll try a bite." Suppose she then took a fork and tasted your food. You would be outraged. You would de-mand to see the manager. You would insist that the food be taken back.

Suppose, however, that you went to a restaurant with your child. When your meal was served, suppose your child said, "That looks delicious! I think I'll try a bite." When your child took a fork and tasted your food, you were not the least bit upset. This is a normal exchange between parent and child.

The difference in the two scenarios is not the words, or even the intent, but the relationship. The parent-child relationship gives boldness and intimacy not available to nonfamily members. The same words take on new meaning in the context of the relationship.

The Scriptures are filled with promises regarding prayer and guidelines regarding relationship.

Personal Prayer Experience

What has been the goal of your prayer life? Has it been to get God to perform for you? How has your goal begun to change? Ask God what He wants to promise you regarding your prayer life. Write down His response.

Search through the Scriptures and find the prayer promises. Write down the promises that mean something specific to you at this time.

REQUIREMENTS OF PRAYER

4-19-95
2:25 a.m.

Prayer and Faith

"'Have faith in God,' Jesus answered. 'I tell you the truth, if anyone says to this mountain, "Go, throw yourself into the sea," and does not doubt in his heart but believes that what he says will happen, it will be done for him. Therefore I tell you, whatever you ask for in prayer, believe that you have received it, and it will be yours'" (Mark 11:22-24).

Faith and prayer are inseparable. Without faith, we cannot please God. Without faith, we cannot hope to see the kingdom of heaven. The Scriptures are uncompromisingly clear. We must have faith. But, what is faith?

Is faith a feeling that can be worked up? Can we stir up our faith by repeating certain Scriptures or phrases over and over? Or by listening to stirring orators? Or by any other method? If so, then people can have faith in things that are not true.

In Lewis Carroll's *Through the Looking-Glass*, Alice has this conversation with the White Queen:

> "Now I'll give you something to believe. I'm just one hundred and one, five months and a day."
> "I can't believe that!" said Alice.
> "Can't you?" the Queen said in a pitying tone. "Try again: draw a long breath, and shut your eyes."
> Alice laughed. "There's no use trying," she said: "one can't believe impossible things."
> "I daresay you haven't had much practice," said the Queen. "When I was your age, I always did it for half-an-hour a day. Why, sometimes I've believed as many as six impossible things before breakfast."

This, of course, is a silly conversation in a make-believe story. Yet it is not far from the way we are sometimes taught to stir up faith. "If only you can believe hard enough," we're told, "you can get God to do anything. Just follow this formula and you can believe anything."

Faith is not believing real hard. Faith is not shutting your eyes and drawing a long breath and willing yourself to believe something. Faith is not a feeling. It is not a currency to be traded in for favors. When we have a mistaken understanding of faith, we tend to spend our time examining our own feelings rather than looking to God. We are depending on our feelings of faith, not on God. True faith points directly to God. Faith is effective because God is faithful. 4. 2

Faith is the ability to live in the spiritual realm. By faith we live out spiritual truth. Faith is part of your spiritual inheritance. It is a gift from God. You cannot stir faith up. Faith is acquired through your spiritual senses.

Spiritual Senses

"Since we live by the Spirit, let us keep in step with the Spirit," says the Apostle Paul in Galatians 5:25. Paul assumes that we are living out the details of our lives according to the prompting and direction of the Spirit. He reminds us to walk in the Spirit's rhythm, not to get out of sync or offbeat. How do we get in step and keep in step with the Spirit? By faith.

When you were born into the physical world, you were born with a set of physical senses. These are the senses by which you interpret, understand, and interact with your physical world. By your senses, you receive knowledge about your world. This knowledge forms the basis of your behavior. For instance, if your sense of hearing tells you that a speeding car is coming at you from behind, you jump out of the way. If your sense of sight tells you that the plant in your window needs to be watered, you water it. If your sense of smell tells you that the milk in the refrigerator has soured, you dispose of it. You base your actions and your beliefs about your physical world on the knowledge transmitted to you by your senses.

You have learned that your physical senses are reliable. Seeing is believing, the saying goes. "I would never have believed it, except I heard it with my own ears," you may have said.

Suppose I'm standing in a room full of people. How would I know the room was full of people? My senses would tell me so. I would see them, hear them, and touch them. Now suppose that someone enters the room, looks around, and says, "There's no one here. This room is empty." Would I believe that person? Of course not. Because I have learned by experience that my senses are reliable and accurate transmitters of knowledge about my world. I would have unwavering faith that the room was full of people. I would believe what my senses told me.

When you were born into the kingdom of God, you were born with a set of spiritual senses.

Taste and see that the Lord is good (Psalm 34:8).

How sweet are your promises to my taste, sweeter than honey to my mouth! (Psalm 119:103).

I pray also that the eyes of your heart may be enlightened in order that you may know (Eph. 1:18).

The Sovereign Lord has opened my ears (Isa. 50:5).

He who has ears, let him hear (Matt. 11:15).

Your spiritual senses are the means by which you know, understand, and respond to your spiritual world. Faith grows as a result of responding to your spiritual senses. "Faith comes from hearing the message, and the message is heard through the word of Christ" (Rom. 10:17). What does this verse mean? Is it talking about the physical sense of hearing? No. The passage is explaining that not everyone who hears the message with physical ears accepts it. The one who hears with spiritual ears, who hears Christ speaking His word at the deepest level, finds faith.

So, then, what is faith? Is faith feeling sure that you can predict what God will do? No. Faith is a gift from God, not earned by works and nothing for anyone to boast about (see Eph. 2:8).

Faith is your God-given capacity to receive and act on spiritual knowledge. "By faith Abraham . . . obeyed" (Heb. 11:8). Your spiritual senses are as reliable and as trustworthy as your physical senses. Your spiritual senses are not feelings, emotions, or fleeting impressions. You can be sure about the knowledge you receive by means of your spiritual senses.

You do not have to find more faith or work up more faith. Your faith will increase as your spiritual senses mature. When a baby is born into the physical world, that baby has the sense of sight, but cannot distinguish and identify shapes. The baby has the sense of hearing, but cannot divide sounds into words and ascribe meaning to them. The baby's senses have to mature over time and with practice. It is the same with your spiritual senses. Knowing how to hear God clearly and reliably is learned by the slow discipline of prayer and obedience. God will guide you gently and steadily. He will open your ears. He will enlighten the eyes of your heart. He will teach you how to keep in step with the Spirit.

The book of 2 Kings records an instance in the life of Elisha that illustrates the difference between using physical senses and using spiritual senses. The king of Syria was angry because Elisha had warned the king of Israel about his plans several times. He decided to ambush Elisha.

> Then he sent horses and chariots and a strong force there. They went by night and surrounded the city. When the servant of the man of God got up and went out early the next morning, an army with horses and chariots had surrounded the city. "Oh, my lord, what shall we do?" the servant asked.
> "Don't be afraid," the prophet answered. "Those who are with us are more than those who are with them."

Elisha's servant, judging by that which his physical senses perceived, was undoubtedly confused. He and Elisha were looking at the same scene and seeing two different situations. As far as he could see, it was him and Elisha against a great army of Syrians. Then came the turning point.

> And Elisha prayed, "O Lord, open his eyes so he may see." Then the Lord opened the servant's eyes, and he looked and saw the hills full of horses and chariots of fire all around Elisha.

God allowed the servant to see with his physical eyes what Elisha saw with his spiritual eyes. The facts of the situation did not change. Only his interpretation of the facts changed. Once his spiritual eyes were opened, he could see not only the facts but the Truth.

Faith comes by seeing with spiritual eyes and hearing with spiritual ears. We have a God-given capacity to receive spiritual information. "The man without the Spirit does not accept the things that come from the Spirit of God, for they are foolishness to him, and he cannot understand them, because they are spiritually discerned. The spiritual man makes judgments about all things" (1 Cor. 2:14-15).

Faith in Action

"Now faith is the substance [assurance] of things hoped for, the evidence [conviction] of things not seen" (Heb. 11:1

KJV). The words used to define faith—*substance, assurance, evidence, conviction*—are substantive words. These words do not describe emotions, but knowledge, reliable information from a reliable Source.

The writer of Hebrews, after giving a definition of faith, goes on to illustrate faith through the lives of faithful people. By using real people, he shows us how faith looks when it's lived out. As examples, he mentions Abel, Enoch, Abraham, Noah, Sarah, Isaac, Jacob, Joseph . . . the list goes on. Faith manifested itself differently in each life. One thing remained constant. In each life, the faith journey began with hearing from God. Faith gave birth to obedience. Those held up as examples of faith were not commended for how they felt. They were commended for what they did based on what they heard from God.

Abraham is mentioned as the prime example of faith. "By faith Abraham, when called to go to a place he would later receive as his inheritance, obeyed and went, even though he did not know where he was going" (Heb. 11:8). Faith began with God calling. When Abraham was called, he obeyed. He knew two things: the goal (a place he was to receive as an inheritance) and the next step (he went out, not knowing where we was going). He did not know every twist and turn in the journey. He did not receive a step-by-step procedure outlining God's plan from beginning to end. By faith, he obeyed the one thing he knew. His faith was not how he felt, but that he heard and obeyed. Faith is not believing something, but believing Someone.

Faith Is Not a Feeling

"And without faith it is impossible to please God" (Heb. 11:6). This does not mean that God is angered or displeased when our emotions fluctuate. It means that anything, no matter how good, done based on our physical senses or human wisdom cannot please God. What gives God pleasure is that which is done in response to His voice, with His strength.

Several times Jesus rebuked the disciples for having little faith. He was not referring to their feelings. He was correcting them for drawing their conclusions based on the perceptions of their physical senses, not their spiritual senses. Our physical senses discern the facts; our spiritual senses discern the Truth.

Matthew 14:22-33 tells us a story about faith that faltered. Jesus had sent His disciples ahead of Him by boat across the lake. Several hours later when the boat was about three miles out, Jesus came toward them, walking on the water. The disciples were terrified, thinking He was a ghost. Jesus called out, "'Take courage! It is I. Don't be afraid.'" Peter, ever the impetuous one, said, "'Lord, if it's you, . . . tell me to come to you on the water.'" Jesus replied, "'Come.'"

Responding to Jesus' voice, not to the circumstances, Peter walked toward Jesus on the water. When Peter changed his focus and responded to the knowledge he received from his physical senses instead of the call of Jesus, he began to sink. "Immediately Jesus reached out his hand and caught him. 'You of little faith,' he said, 'why did you doubt?'"

What was Jesus rebuking Peter about? Could Peter have felt frightened and unsure and still have responded to Jesus' voice instead of to his circumstances? Yes. Jesus was rebuking Peter for reaching his conclusion about his situation based on information from his physical senses rather than revelation from Jesus.

How Does Faith Grow?

As our ability to hear God increases, so does our ability to believe Him. Faith matures as we walk in the Spirit. Faith grows as we invest it. Every believer has been gifted with faith (see Rom. 12:3). Every believer is responsible before God to increase his or her faith by investing, or using, it. We have to risk our faith to see it grow.

Jesus told a parable of a man who was going on a journey and entrusted his possessions to his slaves. To one slave he gave five talents; to another, two; and to another, one. The slaves who had received five and two talents immediately began to invest what they had and to gain more. The slave with one talent, afraid to risk losing what little he had, buried his talent in the ground. He didn't use it. He didn't risk it. It accomplished nothing.

When the master returned, he was angry. He had expected

the same from every slave—to invest and increase what he had been given.

Some of us feel that we have only a tiny, inadequate faith. We're afraid that if we risk our little, weak faith by hearing from God and acting on His word, we might lose what we have. God might let us down and we would be left with no faith at all. So instead of living and praying on the cutting edge of the kingdom of God—instead of investing our faith boldly—we bury it. We play it safe. Finally, we lose what little faith we had.

How can you increase your faith? Invest it. Stop worrying about how little your faith is. Take your eyes off your faith and fix them on Him Who is called Faithful and True. Invest what faith you have. Risk it all on the faithfulness of God. Each time you invest your faith, it will grow. You will have even more faith to invest in the next situation. As you live by the faith you have, it will steadily increase.

Faith, then, is the God-given capacity to live in the spiritual realm. Faith requires that all of your spiritual attention be on God, not on your own faith or lack of faith. Come to Him as a little child. "Let us hold unswervingly to the hope we profess, for he who promised is faithful" (Heb. 10:23).

Personal Prayer Experience

Bring one concern before the Lord. Ask Him through faith to supply all that is needed for that circumstance.

Wait on Him.

Pray as you feel impressed.

Rely on your spiritual senses.

Prayer and Obedience

"Dear friends, if our hearts do not condemn us, we have confidence before God and receive from Him anything we ask, because we obey his commands and do what pleases Him" (1 John 3:21-22). Obedience is essential for prayer.

A H

However, answers to prayer are not rewards for good behavior. Obedience is not a trade-off. "If I do so-and-so, You'll give me what I want." We cannot buy the answers to our prayers with our actions. Obedience is not a bargaining chip; nor is it a way to get God in our debt so that He owes us something. Obedience is not a favor we do for God.

To understand the role of obedience in prayer, we need to put all the pieces together. Prayer is more than the words we say; it is the total relationship in which we live.

Prayer begins with God and achieves its true purpose when it reflects His will. So that we can pray according to His will, He works in us to re-create His own heart. He reproduces His desires in us so that we desire what He wants to give. He has given us the capacity to hear from Him so that we can experience true fellowship with Him. The capacity to hear from Him and to see the unseen results in faith. Without faith it is impossible to please Him.

How does obedience fit in? Disobedience dulls our spiritual senses. Our disobedience doesn't change anything except our ability to perceive spiritual truth. If I was looking at something and removed my glasses, it would not change anything about the situation except my ability to see it clearly. I could still make out vague outlines, but the details would elude me. In my prayer life, this blurring would limit my usefulness as an intercessor because I would not be able to see spiritual reality clearly. I would lose my ability to hear the subtle nuances of His communication. I would miss His whisper.

"'If you had responded to my rebuke, I would have poured out my heart to you and made my thoughts known to you'" (Prov. 1:23). Obedience is the action of faith. Revelation follows obedience. Act on what God has revealed and more revelation will follow. Jesus said, "'Whoever has my commands and obeys them, he is the one who loves me. He who loves me will be loved by my Father, and I too will love him and show myself to him'" (John 14:21). In other words, the one who obeys Me is the one who loves Me. I will show Myself clearly to that one. Obedience will bring revelation.

God wants to give us firsthand revelation. "'I . . . will . . .

show myself to him'" (John 14:21). He is speaking from within. His words are re-creating you. His work within you is causing you to find pleasure in that which gives Him pleasure. He is causing you to desire His will (Phil. 2:13). His words are so close that they are in your heart and in your mouth (Rom. 10:8). That's how much a part of you He is. He wants you to have firsthand knowledge that He "richly blesses all who call on him" (Rom. 10:12). Your obedience allows you to experience Him.

Obedience Brings Freedom

In our society's vernacular, the word *obedience* translates into "burden." We think of obedience as keeping us from being able to do what we want to do. Instead, we have to do what someone else wants us to do. We immediately envision unfulfilled desires, painful sacrifices, drudgery. This view is the direct opposite of the truth. "I will walk about in freedom, for I have sought out your precepts" (Psalm 119:45).

Obedience is freedom. Every command of God's is designed to free us. The command to forgive is to free us from the heavy burden of anger and bitterness. His command to turn the other cheek is to free us from the never-ending obsession to get even, to have the last word. Unrighteousness is a harsh taskmaster. We will destroy ourselves trying to obey its dictates and bear the burdens it thrusts upon us. To accept His yoke is to find rest. "'My yoke is easy and my burden is light'" (Matt. 11:30). The deeper the experience we have of God, the more eagerly we obey. "I run in the path of your commands, for you have set my heart free" (Psalm 119:32).

In order to walk in obedience, we must listen to God. God's communication is not generic. What one person hears from God in a specific situation will not automatically translate to someone else's situation. God's communication to you will be personal and specific. He is intent on getting through to you.

"I will go before you and will level the mountains; I will break down gates of bronze and cut through bars of iron. I will give you the treasures of darkness, riches stored in secret places, so that you may know that I am the Lord, the God of Israel, who calls you by name" (Isa. 45:2-3).

Obedience and prayer are inseparable. Obedience keeps our spiritual senses sharp. God wants our prayers to be the pipeline through which His will flows from the spiritual world to the physical world. Stubborn disobedience, unconfessed sin, or broken relationships are a clog in the pipeline. The power of God cannot flow uninterrupted with all its potential force. A life of obedience is an unclogged pipeline for the will and the kingdom of God.

Sometimes the obedience required is in terms of life-style. Sometimes obedience enters in as God gives a specific command as part of the answer to prayer. Sometimes obedience is to persevere in prayer according to His will until His will is accomplished. There is no book of rules to follow. God will communicate His expectations in the context of a continuous experience of Him and in line with His word. Obedience is living in a permanent state of receptivity and availability to God. The difference between obeying God's voice and acting on your own to "help God out" is the difference between a mind set on what the Spirit desires and a mind set on the human nature. The distinction is subtle and is spiritually discerned.

Personal Prayer Experience

Ask God to show you areas of disobedience. Repent and accept His forgiveness and cleansing. Ask Him to create in you the desire and ability to obey. Record your thoughts.

Prayer and Forgiveness

"'And when you stand praying, if you hold anything against anyone, forgive him, so that your Father in heaven may forgive you your sins'" (Mark 11:25). Failing to forgive anyone anything is closing the door to God. If we, as intercessors, are to be the channels of God's will into the world, we cannot clog the channels with angry memories. Holding on to anger is cutting off the flow of His power through us.

Refusing to forgive others is saying no to God's gracious

offer of forgiveness, not that forgiveness is a tit-for-tat propo-
sition (i.e., if you'll forgive others, He'll forgive you). By
choosing to hold on to anger and bitterness, we are refusing
to repent of that very anger. Repentance opens the door to receive God's free grace.

To forgive does not mean to forget. Our memories remain
intact. Often, erasing a hurt from our memories is a way to
bury it and never face the pain it brings. This is not forgiving.
The first step in forgiving is to acknowledge the anger and
pain. In Christ we do not have to fear memory. No offense,
no matter how vile, can destroy us.

> Who shall separate us from the love of Christ? Shall trouble or
> hardship or persecution or famine or nakedness or danger or
> sword? As it is written: "For your sake we face death all day
> long; we are considered as sheep to be slaughtered." No, in all
> these things we are more than conquerors through him who
> loved us. For I am convinced that neither death nor life, nei-
> ther angels nor demons, neither the present nor the future, nor
> any powers, neither height nor depth, nor anything else in all
> creation, will be able to separate us from the love of God that
> is in Christ Jesus our Lord (Rom. 8:35-39).

This does not mean we will not feel the pain. This does not
mean that it will be easy to walk through the process. (There
are many levels of offense. I am speaking here of those deep,
wrenching hurts such as abuse and betrayal.) Perhaps you
can immediately identify with such phrases as "we face death
all day long" or "we are considered as sheep to be slaugh-
tered." As God walks you toward forgiveness, you will also
understand that "in all these things we are more than con-
querors through him who loved us."

God wants to uncover things that are covered up, to pull
things out of the darkness into the light. There is no need to
pretend. He is Truth. Face your feelings fearlessly, even those
you consider unacceptable. It is not important to have the
"right" feelings all the time, but to direct your feelings to the
right place. Forgiving is a process. As long as you are in the
process, you are walking in the light. "If you possess these
qualities in increasing measure [i.e., they do not have to be
present in their fullness, but they are developing], they will

keep you from being ineffective and unproductive in your knowledge of our Lord Jesus Christ" (2 Pet. 1:8).

The process of forgiving is a matter of individual timing. God has a path for you to walk and a plan for you to follow. Listen to Him. Don't become sidetracked by other people's answers and opinions. Don't let someone else's experience make you feel inadequate. Don't allow the enemy to discourage you by mocking God. His favorite taunt is "'God will not deliver him'" (Psalm 3:2) or "'God has forsaken him; pursue him and seize him, for no one will rescue him'" (Psalm 71:11). Your response to such thoughts is this: "But you are a shield around me, O Lord, my Glorious One, who lifts up my head" (Psalm 3:3).

There are other less-traumatic offenses. They still must be forgiven. Because they are so common, many times we leave them untended and they fester and spread their poison throughout our spirits. The perceived slight, the thoughtless word, the harsh exchange, the cutting comment—one hurt piles on another to erode relationships and diminish the prayer life. This is particularly common between spouses or among family members. If a current offense brings back the memories and anger associated with past offenses, it is time to commit yourself to the forgiving process.

Then there are the minuscule offenses, which still require forgiving: the driver who cut in front of you in traffic, the salesclerk who treated you rudely, the car mechanic who overcharged. That flash of anger signals the need to forgive. Extend to them the mercy you expect others to extend to you.

Forgive as Christ Forgave

Forgiving is the truest experience of dying to self in order to live to God. We are to forgive as God in Christ forgave us (Eph. 4:32). That forgiveness is undeserved and complete. We are to begin the forgiving process before we've won the argument, without having the last word. In order to forgive fully, we must short-circuit the course of our anger. Anger left to take its natural course will cripple your spirit. You will still go through stages of anger; but when anger and hurt are committed to God, you will be working your way out of

anger rather than letting anger take root in your life. \
begin to forgive at the moment of the offense. As the na.
were being pounded in His hands and His feet, Jesus was forgiving. "'Father, forgive them, for they do not know what
they are doing'" (Luke 23:34).

Forgiveness will be accomplished by Christ in you, your
hope of glory. Like everything else He requires, He has already made provision. Let Christ be Christ in you. Release
every experience to Him so that He can make use of it for
your benefit. You are His workmanship. He is building you.
You will know that you have finished the forgiving process
when you can remember the event without feeling the anger.

When you stand praying, then, forgive. Forgive so that you
can be an unclogged channel through whom God can pour
out His mercy, to whom God can grant a spirit of wisdom
and revelation in the knowledge of Him (Eph. 1:17).

Personal Prayer Experience

Ask God to spotlight areas of unforgiveness in your life.
Put yourself in God's hands and commit yourself to the
process of forgiveness. Record your honest thoughts.

Prayer and Authority

Jesus invites us to approach the Father in His name. Consider what that means. The One Who has all authority in
heaven and on earth has authorized us to speak in His name.
To pray in His name means to speak His desires.

When one person gives another the privilege of using his
or her name, it is an indication of trust. It is saying to another,
"Use the credibility I have earned to establish your own. You
will not need to prove yourself in order to have immediate
access to the benefits I have earned because you will be coming in my name and not your own. My reputation will be imputed to you. You will be received as I am."

My earthly parents are wonderful people. I benefit from

their reputations. When I meet someone who has known my parents, that person immediately begins to treat me with a respect I have not earned. The person treats me with the respect he or she has for my parents. The reputation my parents have earned is imputed to me. I am treated as if I had actually done all the generous and loving things that my parents have done simply because I bear their name.

This is the privilege Jesus has given us. We are to approach God in His name. "'I have given them the glory that you gave me'" (John 17:22). The righteousness of Christ is imputed to us because we are His. God receives us with all the love and joy that He receives Jesus with. He delights in us as He delights in Jesus. He loves us the same way He loves Jesus. "'That the love you have for me may be in them and that I myself may be in them'" (John 17:26). What boldness we have before Him.

"Therefore, brothers, since we have confidence to enter the Most Holy Place by the blood of Jesus, by a new and living way which opened for us through the curtain, that is, His body" (Heb. 10:19-20). We are the beneficiaries of His work. He inaugurated the new and living way to the Father; He fulfilled God's requirements; and we can approach God based on what He did on our behalf. "By one sacrifice He has made perfect forever those who are being made holy" (Heb. 10:14).

Original Authority and Delegated Authority

Jesus said, "'And I will do whatever you ask in my name, so that the Son may bring glory to the Father'" (John 14:13). We are to use His name to access His riches to fulfill His purposes through prayer. His one purpose is to glorify God. I am president of a certain organization. As president, I must sign all checks written on that organization's account. By signing a check, I have the authority to access the organization's resources. I do not have authority to use those resources for my own benefit, or for any purposes except those set forth and approved by the membership. My signature releases the organization's resources to carry out the organization's plans. I act in the name of that organization. If I do not exercise the authority delegated to me—if I do not sign checks—the organization's purposes will not be accomplished. In a similar way, Jesus has given us the authority to access His resources for His purposes through prayer. Our God-authored prayers release His riches just like the signature on a check releases the resources in that checking account.

As we live a praying life, His desires become our desires. His life flows through us as the vine's life flows through the branch. He abides in us and we abide in Him. Then we ask for whatever we wish and it is done for us (John 15:4,7). This is our authority in prayer, that we abide in Him and His words abide in us. We are being molded into His image from the inside out by His life in us.

Let's look at the issue of spiritual authority. All authority belongs to Jesus (Matt. 28:18). He is far above all rule and authority and power and dominion. All things are in subjection under His feet and He is head over all things (Eph. 1:22-23). All things were created by Him and for Him. He existed before all things and in Him all things hold together (Col. 1:16-17). "That in all things he might have the preeminence" (Col. 1:18 KJV). Jesus is Lord.

Jesus has original authority. We have delegated authority. Let me illustrate this principle. The President of the United States has original authority. The Constitution gives him that authority. Decisions originate with him. The secretary of state has delegated authority. He negotiates with world leaders and hammers out treaties and agreements in the President's name. He has the full authority to speak for the President as long as he is speaking the President's thoughts, as long as he is being the President's mouthpiece. Were the secretary of state to begin speaking in his own name, as a private citizen, he no longer has any authority. Delegated authority must be backed up by original authority. Delegated authority is only operative when it is the exact representation of the original authority that backs it up.

Another example: One day I was teaching a writing workshop to 165 fourth-graders. I was having trouble because they were not subject to me. I had no authority over them. My words had no effect because I had no authority. The principal walked by and noticed my problem. She came into the room and sat down. Suddenly the situation changed. Now those fourth-graders were subject to me. Suddenly they obeyed every word I said. Why? Because the principal, the original authority, had delegated her authority to me. Because of her presence, the children responded to my words as if they were her words. I exercised her authority. It was as if her words were in my mouth.

Jesus has given us delegated authority backed up by His original authority. Our prayers enforce the authority and lordship of Jesus. Look at it like this: This is a country built on laws. As a citizen of this country, those laws have authority over me. The law says I must drive no faster than 65 miles per hour (MPH) on the interstate highways. I am subject to that law. Does that mean I can't drive faster than 65 MPH? No. I can drive as fast as I want to drive. The law will only affect my situation if someone with authority enforces it, or puts force behind it.

Jesus is Lord. We don't make Him Lord—He is Lord. Everything is subject to Him. By our prayers, we enforce His Lordship—bring it to bear on a specific situation.

Elijah: Standing in the Gap

Elijah is cited as an example of a person who prayed with authority. James reminds us that Elijah was only human, yet his prayers accomplished God's will. "The prayer of a righteous man is powerful and effective. Elijah was a man just like us. He prayed earnestly that it would not rain, and it did not rain on the land for three and one-half years. Again he prayed, and the heavens gave rain, and the earth produced its crops" (James 5:16-18).

Here is what God wants us to learn: Prayer has great power and great effect. For example, Elijah's prayers had so much power and so much effect that they held rain off the earth for three and one-half years, then they released rain onto the earth. To put this teaching in context, we must look at the incident to which it refers.

"Now Elijah the Tishbite . . . said to Ahab, 'As the Lord, the God of Israel, lives, whom I serve, there will be neither dew nor rain in the next few years except at my word'" (1 Kings

17:1). What authority Elijah assumes! No rain will fall except by his word. Where did Elijah get such authority?

We are given two clues as to the source of Elijah's boldness. First, he states his position. He stands before God. He has direct access to Jehovah. Whose idea, then, was it for a drought to occur on the earth? God's or Elijah's? It was God's idea. That's why Elijah had such boldness. He was speaking God's word. From the book of James we learn that Elijah enforced God's word by prayer. "He prayed earnestly that it would not rain."

Second, we learn something about the word of Elijah in 1 Kings 17:24. Elijah has just raised a widow's son from the dead. "Then the woman said to Elijah, 'Now I know that you are a man of God and that the word of the Lord from your mouth is truth.'" Elijah's words are God's words. Elijah did not come to God with the idea of a drought in the land. God spoke His will to Elijah and Elijah spoke it into the world. Elijah was the channel of God's will.

The second part of Elijah's prayer is that the drought would end. "Again he prayed, and the heavens gave rain, and the earth produced its crops." Where does this prayer originate? In the heart of God. "After a long time, in the third year, the word of the Lord came to Elijah: 'Go and present yourself to Ahab, and I will send rain on the land'" (1 Kings 18:1). In response, Elijah said to Ahab, "'Go, eat and drink, for there is the sound of a heavy rain'" (1 Kings 18:41). The sound of a heavy rain was not heard by anyone but Elijah. Why? Because Elijah heard it with his spiritual ears, not his physical ears. Yet he considered his spiritual hearing so reliable that, based on it, he announced that a heavy rain was coming. He was so certain that his spiritual perception was reality that he instructed Ahab to act as if it had already happened. He told Ahab to celebrate the end of the drought.

"So Ahab went off to eat and drink, but Elijah climbed to the top of Carmel, bent down to the ground and put his face between his knees" (1 Kings 18:42). Elijah proceeded to pray until spiritual reality was manifested physically. He prayed until the rain he heard with his spirit could be seen with his eyes. Elijah's prayers were the appointed way of bringing

God's will to earth. Elijah enforced God's word by prayer.

Elijah did not know the details about how God would accomplish His word. He knew what God would do, but not when He would do it. Elijah knew what his part was. He was to pray until he saw God's will done. When he saw a cloud as small as a man's hand coming out of the sea (1 Kings 18:44), he warned Ahab to leave before a heavy rain stopped him. In a tiny cloud, Elijah saw a great thundershower. Another person, seeing the same sight, would not have recognized the end of a three-year drought. But Elijah was alert, watching eagerly for God's work. The eyes of Elijah's heart were enlightened. Through the eyes of faith, a tiny raincloud appears as a drought-ending thundershower.

"Meanwhile, the sky grew black with clouds, the wind rose, a heavy rain came on" (1 Kings 18:45). Elijah was a man with a nature like ours.

The authority we have in prayer is the authority to bind or loose that which has already been bound or loosed in heaven. When Elijah bound rain off the earth, it was because God had proclaimed it so. When Elijah loosed rain on the earth, it was because God had proclaimed it so. We have the authority to proclaim God's will: "Thy kingdom come. Thy will be done in earth, as it is in heaven."

Personal Prayer Experience

Visualize the presence of God on His throne. Enter His presence in Jesus' name. Experience the joy with which He welcomes you.

What concerns you? Bring it to God. In Jesus' name, access the resources of heaven for that concern. 4-24-95

3:05

10 min prayer

RESULTS OF PRAYER 4-29-95   3:28 am.

The longer we live a praying life, the more consistently we walk in faith, the more completely our lives become immersed in His, the more we become like Him. The gap between His will and ours becomes narrower. His life flows from us more spontaneously, with less thought and effort. Our plans come to reflect His purpose. Our desires match His. He is our very great reward.

In the course of the praying life, God reveals His faithfulness. Our eyes become riveted on Him. He becomes the focus of our lives. We are freed from the uncertainty induced by scrutinizing our prayer methods to see if they measure up. Do I have enough faith? Did I pray fervently enough, or long enough, or eloquently enough? Did I present my case with enough passion? In the praying life, we can forget the method and look to the Master. The secret to prayer lies in Him alone.

There are two sides to prayer. "The Lord Almighty has sworn, 'Surely, as I have planned, so it will be, and as I have purposed, so it will stand.' . . . For the Lord Almighty has purposed, and who can thwart him? His hand is stretched out, and who can turn it back?" (Isa. 14:24,27). The absolute sovereignty of God is in apparent contradiction to the choices of our free will. "May he grant you your heart's desire, and fulfil all your plans!" (Psalm 20:4 RSV). In the praying life, the contradictions are resolved. The choices of our free will are shaped by His sovereign plan. His life begins to flow out of us in rivers of living water. "'I have been crucified with Christ and I no longer live, but Christ lives in me. The life I live in the body, I live by faith in the Son of God'" (Gal. 2:20).

Personal Prayer Experience

Listen to God say this to you:

Darling Child:
  I love you without limits. I yearn to pour out My blessing on you. My plans for you are more than you can imagine.
  Look to Me. Lose yourself in My life. Relinquish all trust in yourself, in your ability to pray correctly. I am all you need. Abandon yourself to Me.

THE PROMISE OF PRAYER
REVIEW

Pg. 59

1. The promise of prayer is a _____.
2. Faith is effective because_____ *Pg 61* .
3. Faith is born of _____ not _____.
4. Obedience is essential for prayer, but answers to prayer are not ____*P. 68*___ for good behavior.
5. Disobedience _____ our _____ senses.
6. Is obedience a burden or a freedom? Explain.

7. Refusing to forgive others is saying _____ to God's gracious offer of _____.

8. We are to use Jesus' name to access _____ to fulfill _____. His one purpose is to _____.

9. Jesus has _____ authority. We have _____ authority.

10. The seeming conflict between the sovereignty of God and the choices of our free will is resolved in the praying life. The choices of our _____ are shaped by His _____.

Answers: (1) transformed heart; (2) God is faithful; (3) revelation, information; (4) rewards; (5) dulls, spiritual; (6) obedience frees us from the burdens imposed on us by our human nature; (7) no, forgiveness; (8) His riches, His purpose, glorify God; (9) original, delegated; (10) free will, sovereign plan.

THE PRACTICE OF PRAYER

The pursuit of any goal requires a narrowed focus. To hold fast to one goal means to dismiss many others. The pursuit of any goal demands single-minded diligence. In the pursuit of God, we find within ourselves the desire to divest ourselves of anything that may slow our progress and to run unencumbered toward the goal.

The pursuit of any goal requires a narrowed focus. To hold fast to one goal means to dismiss many others. The pursuit of any goal demands single-minded diligence. We must be willing to sacrifice anything not related to our firmly established goal. In the pursuit of God we must evaluate life, not in terms of the technicalities of right and wrong but Does this push me toward my goal or distract me from my goal? As God works to reproduce His heart in us, we will find that many things that are not technically "wrong" are still encumbrances that keep us from effectively running toward the goal. We find within ourselves the desire to divest ourselves of anything that may slow our progress. What may seem all right to a more casual seeker will be forbidden to us. Willingly, joyfully, we lay aside every weight. The One Who is calling us "by his own glory and goodness" (2 Pet. 1:3) is so compelling that our sacrifice feels like privilege. What we once considered gain, we now see as loss. What we once counted as treasure, we now know is rubbish.

> But whatever was to my profit I now consider loss for the sake of Christ. What is more, I consider everything a loss compared to the surpassing greatness of knowing Christ Jesus my Lord, for whose sake I have lost all things. I consider them rubbish, that I may gain Christ (Phil. 3:7-8).

The praying life is a life of diligence. In the praying life, we welcome Him as the refiner's fire, burning away every distraction. To the physical ears such a call sounds harsh and unappealing. To the ears of faith it is like a "perfume poured out" (Song of Songs 1:3). The heart of the seeker responds, "Show me your face, let me hear your voice; for your voice is sweet, and your face is lovely" (Song of Songs 2:14).

Personal Prayer Experience

Ask God to show you anything that is slowing your progress toward your goal. Write down His responses.

Declare your determination to forsake what He has shown you. Claim His power and authority in Jesus' name.

Make this declaration yours:

> My goal is God Himself. Joyfully I lay aside every encumbrance. I commit myself to uncompromising obedience to His Life within me.
>
> Signed _____
>
> Dated _____

TIMES OF PRAYER

A praying life cannot be scheduled. It flows. Yet specific times of uninterrupted prayer must be scheduled. Disciplined prayertimes merge into and become part of the praying life. Jesus gave guidance about structuring our prayertimes. "'When you pray, go into your room, close the door and pray to your Father, who is unseen. Then your Father, who sees what is done in secret, will reward you'" (Matt. 6:6).

The Habit

"'When you pray, . . .'" We must have the habit of praying. A habit is an action that has become fixed in one's life through repetition. The decision to perform a habit is settled. I do not have to decide, for example, whether I will brush my teeth every morning. It is a habit. Long ago I made the decision that I would always brush my teeth in the morning and I fixed it in my life through repetition. I do not struggle every morning with the decision to brush my teeth. I made that decision because I was convinced of the importance of brushing my teeth.

My children brush their teeth every morning, but it is not yet a habit. I have to remind them. They often try to find excuses not to brush their teeth. It is an issue every morning. They do not see the value in brushing their teeth every morning and have no personal commitment to it. Every morning they have to make a decision to brush their teeth.

Scheduled periods of prayer should become our habit. If we are convinced of the value of daily prayertimes, we should begin to fix that action in our lives through repetition. When attempting to establish a new habit, it is important to never allow an exception to occur and to begin the new practice immediately. The decision to rise early for extended prayertime turns on a few seconds. The first seconds after the alarm clock rings will decide your commitment. "As a door turns on its hinges, so a sluggard turns on his bed" (Prov. 26:14). Will you be sluggish or diligent? Will you choose sleep or prayer?

> I went past the field of the sluggard, past the vineyard of the man who lacks judgment; thorns had come up everywhere, the ground was covered with weeds, and the stone wall was in ruins. I applied my heart to what I observed and learned a lesson from what I saw (Prov. 24:30-32).

This is a description of the life of a sluggard. The prayer life, left unattended, is overgrown with weeds, broken down, in disrepair. A praying life requires diligence, or spiritual poverty will sneak up on you and overcome you.

In contrast, God wants to make your life like a watered garden. He wants to tend, protect, and maintain it Himself. "'I, the Lord, watch over it; I water it continually. I guard it day and night so that no one may harm it'" (Isa. 27:3).

When morning comes, don't choose "a little sleep, a little slumber." Don't turn on your bed the way a door turns on its hinge. Instead, get up and spend time with the Father. Let Him tend and water your life. Let Him make it lush with the Spirit's fruit.

To fix a habit, we should not consider the action an option. When the alarm clock goes off, keep moving. Don't allow yourself one minute or five minutes to decide whether you will get up this morning for prayer. The decision is fixed, now fix the behavior. Within five minutes of getting up, the difficulty is over.

Many people find it helpful to do stretching exercises and have a cup of coffee. Some people shower and dress in order to wake up before sitting down to pray. Some people have covenanted with a prayer partner to call at the appointed time in the morning to encourage them to get up. Some people put their alarm clock across the room or in the hall-way so they will have to get out of bed to turn it off.

Although the decision to get up early every morning for prayer may seem overwhelming at first, it will soon become a habit. It will be a normal part of your routine. You will not have to struggle with it morning by morning.

If your life-style or schedule is such that early morning is not an option for scheduled prayertimes, let God show you what time of the day you are to set aside for Him. Keep that appointment diligently. Your scheduled prayertime should not be a burden, but a delight. It is not a "law," but it needs to be a firm commitment.

The Place

"'When you pray, go into your room, close the door . . .'" As part of establishing the habit of daily prayer, we should, as often as possible, use the same location. By choosing a des-ignated location, you have one less decision to make. You can have your Bible and prayer journal, or whatever materials you use, already in place. The more routine the outward be-haviors are, the more energy is focused on the inward activi-ties. When you don't have to give thought to the functional details, you will come to prayer less distracted, more ready to see the unseen.

When you enter into your inner room, you are to shut the door. You need to choose a place where life's distractions will be less likely to infringe. I have a friend who has her prayer-time in her car in the garage. It is also the time of day, early morning, which helps you shut the door on distractions.

Your location should not become so important that you feel you can miss your prayertime if you are away from it.

Your true inner room is within you, at that altar which God has prepared in your spirit, where the aroma of Christ always rises before Him.

The Focus

"'When you pray, . . . pray to your Father, who is unseen.'" The purpose of your prayertime is to give God your undivided attention. It is not for the purpose of securing His favor for the day. His favor rests on you forever. A morning prayertime should not be viewed superstitiously. "When I have a prayertime, my day goes well. When I skip it, I have a bad day." Morning prayer is not a magic powder to sprinkle on your day. If you have a habit of morning prayer, it will be followed by both good and bad days. The difference will be that you will be centered in God and will react differently to both good and bad.

The focus of your prayertime is God Himself. This is not your one chance to get His attention. You will be walking in prayer day and night. It is not critical that you have time to make all of your prayer requests at this time, although you may do so. The agenda for morning prayertime is to hear God, to reaffirm His rule in your life. "He wakens me morning by morning, wakens my ear to listen like one being taught. The Sovereign Lord has opened my ears, and I have not been rebellious; I have not drawn back" (Isa. 50:4-5).

The focus of your prayertime is your Father, Who is unseen. Your prayertime is for His purposes, not for the admiration of people. Jesus warned against those who wanted their prayer lives to be known and admired. While we will probably not pray loudly on the street corners to be seen by others, we may find many ways to tell others how faithful we are to our morning devotions, or how long we prayed this morning. There are reasons to talk about your prayer life, but watch your motives.

The Response

"'Your Father, who sees what is done in secret, will reward you.'" Jesus said that those who pray for the admiration of others would have the reward they seek. Their spiritual lives may

well be applauded and admired. However, they will have settled for a cheap reward. They will not be rewarded with the
presence of God. Theirs will be a perishable crown.

The reward God offers is Himself. And that will be more
than enough. In His presence we will find everything we are
looking for.

Personal Prayer Experience

Write out your personal commitment to fix prayer as a
habit in your life. Sign and date it.

FORMS OF PRAYER

"'And when you pray, do not keep on babbling like pa-
gans, for they think they will be heard because of their many
words'" (Matt. 6:7). An avalanche of words will not move
God. It is not the cry of the lips, but the cry of the heart that
God hears.

Many people are intimidated by the thought of praying for
extended periods of time. "I can't imagine praying for a
whole hour. What would I say?" We don't need to come to
God with our approach mapped out. Not knowing what to
say will relieve the petitioner of one barrier to true prayer: a
predetermined agenda. We do not need to come to Him with
a planned speech. Habakkuk approached God this way: "I
will stand at my watch and station myself on the ramparts; I
will look to see what he will say to me, and what answer I am
to give to this complaint" (Hab. 2:1).

Though we are not to use meaningless repetition to fill in
the blank places, that does not mean that prayers cannot be
repeated. Jesus prayed the same thing three times in the garden of Gethsemane. Paul asked three times that the thorn in
his flesh be removed. There is a difference between perseverance in prayer and meaningless repetition. In meaningless
repetition, the same requests or phrases are repeated hoping

that God will be worn down by our persistence and finally give in to our desires. In persevering prayer, we come repeatedly before the Father until our spirit receives an answer. Persevering prayer overcomes spiritual forces opposed to the will of God. The key to extended times of prayer is not much speaking, but much listening.

Jesus gave further instruction about the form our times of prayer should take.

> After this manner therefore pray ye: Our Father which art in heaven, Hallowed be Thy name. Thy kingdom come. Thy will be done in earth, as it is in heaven. Give us this day our daily bread. And forgive us our debts, as we forgive our debtors. And lead us not into temptation, but deliver us from evil: For thine is the kingdom, and the power, and the glory, for ever. Amen (Matt. 6:9-13 KJV).

Jesus gave a simple outline for disciplined prayertimes. I have found that by following this structure, I can keep my mind on track.

Praise

By beginning prayertimes with praise, we immediately put the spotlight in the right place. The focus of our prayertimes is to be God. As we spend time considering Him, reflecting on His greatness, we build a foothold for our faith. Against the backdrop of His majesty, life takes on its proper perspective.

In Jesus' prayer outline, we are reminded of the relationship on which prayer is built. We approach God as Father. God, we find, is not a demanding taskmaster or an unapproachable sovereign. He is our Father, our daddy, the kind of daddy we long for. Yet He is clothed with splendor and majesty. He is covered with light as with a cloak. He commands the morning and causes the dawn to know its place. He is great in wisdom and mighty in deed. For Him, all the morning stars sang together and all the sons of God shouted for joy. The idols tremble at His presence and the heart of His enemies melt within them. Great is the Lord. He is to be greatly praised.

Praise the Lord, O my soul; all my inmost being, praise his holy name. Praise the Lord, O my soul, and forget not all his benefits (Psalm 103:1-2).

Intercession

Jesus invites us to pray the kingdom and will of God into each situation. Exodus 28:29-30 gives a wonderful description of intercession.

"Whenever Aaron enters the Holy Place, he will bear the names of the sons of Israel over his heart on the breastpiece of decision as a continuing memorial before the Lord. Also put the Urim and Thummin in the breastpiece, so they may be over Aaron's heart whenever he enters the presence of the Lord. Thus Aaron will always bear the means of making decisions for the Israelites over his heart before the Lord."

Intercession is to carry those in need over our hearts before the Lord continually. God will engrave the names of those for whom we are to diligently intercede on our hearts. We cannot be an earnest intercessor for every need. We must allow God to give us intercession assignments. We can briefly bring before the Lord any need we hear of, but prolonged intercession will be assigned by God.

Intercession must be God-authored. We must listen and respond as God places His desires on our hearts. We have been appointed to be the channels of His will and His power in those lives and situations with which He burdens us. We cannot simply run into His presence with a list of demands for how we think the lives of our loved ones should proceed. To be powerful, effective intercessors, we must let Him form our requests. The beginning point of intercession is always, "Thy kingdom come. Thy will be done." Intercession requires as much listening as talking.

Petitions and Supplications

Jesus tells us to come to our loving Father with our daily needs. "Give us this day our daily bread." This simple prayer is all that is required to access the riches of God on our behalf. Throughout history He has shown Himself as the God Who provides. Jesus gave His disciples specific instructions not to be anxious about their daily needs (Matt. 6:25-34). He assures us that our Father knows and cares about our needs. He pointed out that non-Christians are consumed by these concerns and this defines their lives, but we are free of such bondage. He wants us free of worry so that we can focus our energies on Him and His kingdom.

God, our Creator, knows what we need even before we ask Him. He has everything prepared and available to meet those needs. Our prayers will release His resources in our lives. We are not to be anxious, but instead to ask God for daily provision.

God is practical. He created and ordered the universe. He knows and cares about your daily needs. He is watching over you so carefully that He knows how many hairs are on your head. He knows about your need before you do. Before you ever felt your need, God had prepared an answer to it.

Confession

God requires holiness. He requires a clean and uncluttered heart. "Forgive us our debts, as we forgive our debtors." As we approach God in confession, it is a time for Him to shine His holy light on our hearts and lives, examining both motives and actions. Confession is not an exercise in self-loathing. It is a time to let God search our hearts.

It is not our duty to find our faults and tell God about them. It is His place to show us the dark corners. Our part is to confess and forsake what God shows us as our faults and shortcomings. We need to open our lives to Him for His inspection so that He can bring conviction.

> Search me, O God, and know my heart; test me and know my anxious thoughts. See if there is any offensive way in me, and lead me in the way everlasting (Psalm 139:23-24).

When we feel that we are to dredge up our faults for confession, we are focused in the wrong place. We are looking at ourselves when we should be looking at God. Several things can happen. One, we may become so discouraged that we feel unworthy of God's love. One of Satan's most effective ploys is to accuse and condemn. He loves to load us down with a sense of failure and hopelessness. The Holy Spirit's conviction is different from the enemy's condemnation. Two, we may become proud of how humble we are. Three, we may mask the true sin by concentrating on a symptom. We may repent of an action, when it is an underlying attitude that needs cleansing. Our hearts are wicked and deceitful and who can know them? We cannot trust our own hearts and must look to God for truth.

God brings what was hidden into the light. We agree with Him and confess our sins. He forgives us and cleanses us from all unrighteousness (1 John 1:5-10).

We ask God to forgive us, cancel our debt, as we forgive those who have offended us. One area that will be brought into the light is an unforgiving spirit. If we are walking in the light—no dark, hidden corners—we are walking in unbroken fellowship with others. This requires a consistent exchange of mercy and forgiveness between believers. "If we walk in the light, as he is in the light, we have fellowship with one another" (1 John 1:7). Remember, however, that there are many deep, wounding hurts for which forgiveness is a process that moves us toward healing. There are hurts that have left deep scars which may take a lifetime to heal. He will walk us step-by-step through the process. He will not withhold Himself because we have not reached the conclusion. He is not aloof from our struggles. He is overflowing with mercy and grace.

Spiritual Warfare

"'And lead us not into temptation, but deliver us from the evil one'" (Matt. 6:13). All prayer is spiritual warfare. Every prayer that gains ground for God's kingdom loses ground for the enemy. To pray is to be locked in battle with spiritual forces. Spiritual warfare is not a single type of praying. Prayer is warfare.

In 1991 the nation of Iraq invaded and occupied its neighbor to the south, the nation of Kuwait. Iraq occupied territory that did not belong to it. In spiritual warfare, the same thing is true. Satan and his forces are occupying territory that belongs to Jesus.

After the Iraqi invasion of Kuwait, the world community

determined that this aggression would not stand and began to prepare to invade and liberate the occupied territory. The weeks and months before the invasion much propaganda came out of Iraq which was intended to intimidate and dishearten the troops. We heard that Iraqi soldiers were well trained, highly disciplined, loyal, and highly motivated. When the liberating troops actually invaded, they found quite a different thing. They found Iraqi soldiers waiting for the forces to arrive so they could surrender. They were already defeated.

This is a picture of spiritual warfare. Satan's forces are already defeated. Satan was defeated at the cross. "Having disarmed the powers and authorities, he made a public spectacle of them, triumphing over them by the cross" (Col. 2:15).

Satan's only weapon against the intercessor is propaganda. He wages a propaganda campaign tailor-made for you in order to keep you from invading and driving him out of territory he has occupied. His propaganda may be:

> "I don't have time to pray today. I'll be sure to pray tomorrow."

> "Prayer has never worked for me before. Why should I think it will work now?"

> "God doesn't need my prayers. Someone else will do it."

Whatever his propaganda, it is meant to keep you from invading and persevering until the battle is won. If you will enter the battle, you will find Satan and his forces defenseless against you.

Another thing we learned about during the war with Iraq was "smart bombs." These are computer-driven bombs that hit a precise target. These smart bombs don't land in the general area of the target, they actually go through a window or down an elevator shaft. They are exact.

As Satan has occupied territory, he has built strongholds, or fortresses. He has built these fortresses out of arguments and pretensions that set themselves up against the knowledge of God. Think of your Spirit-directed prayers as smart bombs landing on enemy strongholds. Your persevering prayers are systematically and precisely destroying Satan's hold.

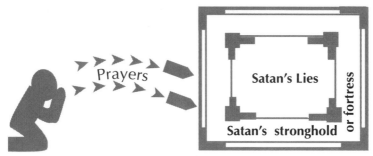

Satan's lies are protected by a fortress built of pretensions that set themselves up against the knowledge of God. His strongholds preserve his lies by keeping them from being exposed to the truth.

God has prepared us for battle through Christ. Every piece of armor described by Paul in Ephesians 6:13-18 is Christ. He is truth. He is righteousness. He is the gospel of peace. He is the source of our faith. He is our salvation. He is the word of God. We are fully protected and armed through Jesus Christ. "For all of you who were baptized into Christ have been clothed with Christ" (Gal. 3:27). We do not require any piece of armor or any weapon outside of Him. "Your life is now hidden with Christ in God. When Christ, who is your life, appears, then you also will appear with him in glory" (Col. 3:3-4).

Jesus' prayer outline teaches us to ask for deliverance from evil or from the evil one. He does not mean deliver in the sense of deliverance of demonic possession, but rescue us from the lies and distortions of the evil one. Satan's tactics are called wily schemes. He is depicted as a master of disguises, wrapping himself in robes of light. He is a master of propaganda meant to break your morale and dilute your resolve. To counter his schemes, we must be well acquainted with the truth. His approach from the beginning has been to distort the truth, to make his lies seem perfectly reasonable. Jesus said that He Himself is the truth (John 14:6). It is by living prayer that the enemy's schemes will be exposed and we will be delivered from his lies.

Personal Prayer Experience

Using Matthew 6:9-13 as an outline, spend one hour in prayer.

THE PRACTICE OF PRAYER
REVIEW

1. The pursuit of any goal requires a _____.

2. The four elements of a disciplined daily prayertime are:

- _____

- _____

- _____

- _____

3. Begin prayertimes with praise in order to spotlight _____.

4. Does God care about your daily needs?

5. Why should we not feel responsible for dredging up our own faults?

6. All prayer is _____.

Answers: (1) narrowed focus; (2) habit, place, focus, response; (3) God's power; (4) yes; (5) we may be listening to the enemy's condemnation, we may become proud of our humility, we may focus on an action when God wants to deal with the attitude; (6) spiritual warfare.

CONCLUSION

These thoughts about prayer are not the result of an intellectual search or theological research. These are my experiences of God, formed in the crucible of my life. Through many painful experiences and deep valleys, God has patiently and gently laid claim to my heart. I have found my resting place, my strong tower.

I have much left to learn about prayer and much left to learn about God. I delight in the journey. He is always new. I delight in the freedom to quit following rules and instead follow Him. I delight in being stretched beyond my limits, to reach toward eternity. But there is more. "'And these are but the outer fringes of his works; how faint the whisper we hear of him! Who then can understand the thunder of his power?'" (Job 26:14). I delight in the discoveries that lie ahead.

I pray this prayer for you, reader:

I pray . . . that the eyes of your heart may be enlightened in order that you may know the hope to which he has called you, the riches of his glorious inheritance in the saints, and his incomparably great power for us who believe (Eph. 1:18-19).